$1.00

MY JOB—
PREACHING

SAMPLES FOR PREACHERS
AND LAYMEN

By
BURRIS JENKINS

COKESBURY PRESS
NASHVILLE, TENN.

MY JOB—PREACHING: SAMPLES FOR
PREACHERS AND LAYMEN. COPYRIGHT
MCMXXXII, BY WHITMORE & SMITH

SET UP, ELECTROTYPED, PRINTED, AND BOUND
BY THE PARTHENON PRESS AT NASHVILLE
TENNESSEE, UNITED STATES OF AMERICA

O

CONTENTS

I

MY JOB—PREACHING

It pleased God by the foolishness of preaching to save them that believed.   1 Corinthians 1: 21.

Someone making a survey of high schools concerning anticipated future employment reported that whenever he asked an assembly of boys and girls how many intended to be farmers, they always laughed and two or three timidly held up their hands. When he asked how many intended to be preachers, they laughed uproariously and nobody held up his hand. Yet there are more men and women engaged in farming than in any other one thing, perhaps than in all other things; and probably there will continue to be as long as humanity lives physically on the fruits of the soil. Always, too, there will be preaching as long as people do not live by bread alone but hunger for something else intangible.

Phillips Brooks used to say that when a young man first began to preach he wondered why everybody didn't come to hear him, but that later on he wondered why anybody did. Nevertheless, the old saying, make a better lead pencil or a better sermon than your neighbor and the

7

world will make a beaten pathway to your door,
stands just as true as it ever did. We may not
understand why, and it may all be foolishness,
still people want to hear preaching, seem to
need to hear preaching, in many instances seem
to be saved by preaching. Men will continue to
preach, therefore, as long as men continue to
aspire.

Styles must change, however, in preaching as
in most things else, with changing times. If it
is true that the thoughts of men are widened
with the process of the suns, then it must follow
that those who preach to widening minds must
widen their messages. No man can tell another
how he ought to preach; no man can even tell
another how he himself goes about it; but certain self-evident facts stand out, certain ele-
mentary principles. And it appears to me that
the very first of these connects up with the
changing of time. The preacher must begin
where the people are, with the things the people
are talking about and thinking of. He makes a
mistake right at the start if he begins with
something remote, something out of harmony
with present-day interests. He must grasp
thoroughly the very first of pedagogical principles, the principle of apperception—that is,
taking hearers where they stand and leading
them gradually on to where they ought to stand.

Jesus showed himself a past master in this

Here may be injected a second principle, that all public speech, to be effective, must be concrete, vivid, picturesque. In a college lecture room, possibly in a parliament, and less probably in a court room, one may dare to be abstract, philosophical. In a pulpit one may venture upon the abstruse only for a very short time and only at his peril. Henry Ward Beecher, although he grappled with the profoundest themes, schooled himself from his very beginnings in concrete and picturesque speech. He tried to think in pictures and to keep always before his hearers pictures, pictures, pictures. He used to say that when he found his congregation growing indifferent, he took them to the country. Pictures can always be seen in the country, cows, horses, chickens, wells, things that people cannot see in town and many of them things they remember from their childhood. One can wake up a city audience with city sights provided one sees them first and points them out to eyes that have only dimly seen them hitherto. All the complex life of our city streets provides pictures for the use of preachers. You can find them in newspapers, chain stores, cafeterias, soda-jerkers, cabarets, jazz orchestras, saxophones, "hominy," adding machines, typewriters, push buttons, and bells.

Humanity forever furnishes pictures, the most interesting in the world, known and read

of all men. We have only to see clearly enough
the ways and the manners, the lives, the com-
edies and tragedies, of men and women and re-
tell them, to catch the public ear and reach the
public heart. We may learn how to do this from
an expert newspaper man who has a nose for
news and fondness for humanity. Ray Stan-
nard Baker, under the pen name of David Grayson, has a series of books called "Adventures"
in various realms, which are only bundles of
human photographs—the Scotch preacher, the
iceman, the little janitor, the bootblack, the millionaire. You and I have people like that round
us all the time. We need only the reporter's
instinct and training to see them and tell about
them. The people will respond.

Most men of experience in the pulpit have
found it necessary to throw away many of the
rules given in the seminary. Rules hinder freedom, cramp and confine personality; and the
very essence of preaching is the projection of
personality. For example, they used to tell us
in the seminary never to use the first personal
pronoun, and never to relate personal experiences—never to say, "A man said to me last
week," or "I knew a man or saw a man or went
fishing with a man or sat at the bedside of a
man who said and did so-and-so." Only one
thing to do to a rule like that, and that is to
throw it away. You can put a congregation to

sleep by obeying that rule; and you can wake a congregation up by disobeying it. Suppose your sermon turns out to be not quite so good a literary product. What of it? Are you after literary products or after the attention and finally the hearts of men and women? Only one rule I know deserves keeping and that is the rule, "Use as perfect English as you can." Even that rule sometimes needs breaking deliberately, for a choice bit of slang or a colloquialism. Beecher used to say also, "When the English language gets in the way of my thought, so much the worse for the English language." That is an attitude which, in my judgment, none but a Beecher can quite dare to assume. The pulpit becomes immensely more powerful if it gains reputation as an authority in pure English.

Another change in the style of our time is the change to a scientific attitude of mind and scientific habits of thinking. Even the untrained masses have caught the contagion and have fallen into the way of reaching conclusions by the inductive method. No longer can we effectively hand down authoritative statements to a questioning and skeptical world. All authorities, these days, stand a bombardment of interrogation. No use in saying to men to-day, "The Bible says so-and-so," or "The Church says so-and-so," or "Religion says so-and-so."

The Bible, the Church, and religion, all these are under investigation by the scientific method. The facts are marshaled from all directions, placed side by side, examined from all angles, and then and only then deductions are drawn, conclusions are reached. Far wiser, then, when wishing to clinch a statement of Bible, church, or religion, to begin patiently and concretely to assemble the facts, to make the pictures, and slowly, gradually to lead up to the generalization. No man gets anywhere to-day, not even in his own family, let alone his own congregation, by dogmatizing. Dogma went out with oil lamps and water jars carried on the head.

It follows as the night the day that the modern mind has little interest in the sectism, the denominationalism, of two or three generations ago, which grew out of dogma. Something of the old atmosphere lingers; and each denomination has a vocabulary, a set of shibboleths, a set of beliefs and traditions, which are all but unintelligible to anybody outside the rank. To hear those who were brought up in one of these denominations holding an intimate conversation concerning the affairs of that particular household of faith is almost like listening to a group talking in a foreign tongue. This nomenclature, the freemasonry of one's own sect, easily creeps into the pulpit. Immediately the preacher alienates the man in the street. He

doesn't give a rap for the denomination; he
grows impatient with the passwords of sectism.
He wants to take up his hat and coat and get
out of there. Only courtesy sometimes holds
him in his seat, and he does not come back.
This world wants religion; and to-day, rather
more than any day in my knowledge, I believe,
it wants Christ, simple, plain, and clear, freed
from all dogmas and sects and petty limitations. It would gladly welcome him, and it will
gladly listen to men who make him clear, under-
standable, living, and breathing.

This leads us to another principle, the necessity for sympathy. To preach effectively one
must have lived as men live, must have had the
joys and the sorrows that men have, must have
walked the same road, easy and hard, that men
have had to walk. Just as no singer can attain
the highest degree of artistry until he or she
has suffered, has known a broken heart, has met
drama and tragedy in life face to face and en-
acted it, so can no preacher reach the hearts of
his fellow men with comfort, with courage, with
inspiration to get up and go on and achieve,
unless he himself has suffered. One of the
greatest preachers in America at this hour, so
one of his most intimate friends tells me, lacks
only this one thing to make him supreme, to
place him where Beecher and Brooks once
stood, a prince of the pulpit. He has not suf-

fered. His life has ever gone in pleasant places, unbroken, placid, prosperous. He has never bowed beneath the storm of obloquy, never writhed under the pain that men know in their darkest hour. Therefore his song misses that minor note of deep and profound fellowship of suffering. Joseph Parker, I think it was, late in life declared that if he had his work to do over again, he would talk more to the broken-hearted. Let a wide and deep tide flow out from the pulpit, of sympathy, of understanding, of desire to help and to heal, to encourage and uplift those whose hearts are bleeding and sore, and a profound response will follow. So few can understand, so few can sympathize, so few can help us in a lonely world, lonely even though packed with crowds, that people instantly will want to touch the hem of the garment of any man who seems to understand.

After all, the old world has not changed, only the dress of it, only the styles of it, only the customs of it. The demand rings out for the same old messages, clothed in a different garb and cut on a different pattern, that Amos and Hosea, Isaiah and Jeremiah, Jesus and Paul proclaimed so many hundreds of years ago. Preach those messages, and men still will tell you they do not want to hear them. Still they will say, "Let the preacher stick to the Bible. Let him preach the good old dogmas. What

business has he dealing with industry, states-
craft, foreign relations, peace and war?''
Those are exactly the things the prophets from
Isaiah down to Paul rang the changes on.
Those are exactly the things that the American
preacher of to-day, over protest and criticism,
must continue to thunder. No age ever needed
them worse. Ours to refuse to be muzzled, to
equivocate, to compromise, to back water and
to shilly-shally, to soft pedal and to conciliate.
Use adroitness and finesse? To be sure. All
the skill, all the delicacy, all the expert per-
formance of apperception that we can muster,
certainly; but let nobody put the bridle on the
pulpit; let nobody from outside of it try to boss
the job. Prophets cannot live with bridles and
blinders on.

No age ever needed that old message hurled
into its teeth more than this age needs it. The
golden rule in business. A fair, square, and
honest chance to work for every man who wants
to work. A just and decent wage and standard
of living for every worker and farmer in the
land. Fraternity and comity among business
houses, banks, stores, shops, and factories. Co-
operation in place of cutthroat competition.
Business leaders dimly begin to discern that
these principles only can lead us out of depression, can save the modern world. Time for
preachers to strike while the iron is hot, to

preach the economics of Jesus, the ethics of the Nazarene, the spirit of the peacemaker, Christ instead of Mars. We shall meet with hostility, if we attempt this high task, just as Isaiah met it, and Jeremiah and Paul and Jesus. Use all the subtlety we may, and be just as diplomatic as we choose, we shall meet the world-old spirit that strains at gnats and swallows camels. The time calls for courage on the part of all public men. Especially it calls for courage on the part of preachers, for they alone stand avowedly for that system of ethics, of economics, and of international relations which can save the world, the system of Jesus.

A big job, this foolishness of preaching. Sometimes we feel the futility of it just because we do not comprehend the bigness of it. How delicate and fine an art, to take people in the midst of their everyday concerns and gently lead them on from the things they play with to the greater things they ought to attain! How much study and thought it demands to keep always a series of pictures flashing before the minds of hearers, Sunday after Sunday, pictures freighted with significance and world-wide importance. How essential not merely that a man practice what he preach, but that he be what he preach! If preaching is the projection of personality, if, as Father Taylor said, "The business of the preacher is to take something hot out of his own heart and shove it into mine," then first of all he must try to live inside himself the light that he tries to throw. No man can tell another how to do it. Each man must be himself, himself and himself alone, sublimated, refined, incandescent with his message. The preacher, unlike other artists, can leave no pictures or symphonies or buildings behind. Like the actor, when he passes off the stage, there is nothing he can leave. His personality has gone. His published words can never be himself. This scientific time calls for scientific methods of treatment. This perplexed, bewildered, and painful time calls for sympathy and understanding and encouragement. Never was a day which more needed this foolishness of preaching; for the same old world staggers along because it will not learn the simple rudiments of life, gentleness, kindness, love, the golden rule, the beauty of service, the willingness to sacrifice and to die for the truth, all the things which Jesus taught.

God. We mumbled prayers and incantations to placate this fearful individual; and if by any chance we forgot the prayer night or morning, we felt assured that something dire would happen to us in the near future.

Now all that is changed. Man has grown so much smaller and the universe so much bigger —and its Creator bigger in proportion—that we can no longer think in the old terms. We find out what a very small speck of dust our earth represents among the myriad worlds. Our solar system, like a puff of cigarette smoke, circles round in a vast galaxy made up of other solar systems as far flung as the Milky Way and farther. The farthest star in this galaxy shines so far away that light, traveling at the rate of 186,000 miles a second, is just reaching us now which started before the Norman conquest, before the pyramids were built, indeed before man inhabited the earth. The mind reels before such distances. To conceive of the rapidity of light, compare it with the radio, which seems to us instantaneous. Light waves and radio waves make the same speed. Sound waves travel more slowly, as we well know. If I were talking into a microphone this morning, I would be heard in Oklahoma or in Iowa more quickly than by those sitting in the rear seats of this church. A concert given in a great hall in New York and radiocast, would be heard in the West Indies or

South America more quickly than by the people
sitting in the hall. Now light, traveling just
that fast, has taken longer than five hundred
millions of years to travel to us from the remot-
est star in our own little neighborhood galaxy
in the sky. Out beyond that galaxy circle and
sweep hundreds and thousands of other similar
galaxies that we have never seen, perhaps never
shall see. There is no end to space, although
Einstein advances the theory that space circles
round upon itself just as a traveler on this globe
circles round upon himself if he goes on long
enough. Before such theory the mind breaks
down. The point is, though, that God made all
that. He is bigger than six feet.

Turn the eyes the other way, not through the
telescope but the microscope. The last fifty
years have revealed a world just as stupendous,
although infinitesimal, in this other direction.
The molecule we have known of for some time.
For a long while we thought it the smallest
form of matter. Small enough in all conscience!
And yet everlastingly energetic. Molecules
forever go whizzing through space at the speed
of a rifle ball. Even those in foundation stones
are moving at such a rate, and those in water.
If you want to increase their speed, heat up a
little water, drive it off in the form of steam,
and the molecules then go traveling faster than
any rifle ball across battle fields. They bump

into each other, too, and go bounding off in all
directions. Numberless such rifle balls, pounding on a piston, drive our trains across the continent. Yet these molecules have now been divided into atoms, and the atoms into electrons,
like the positive and negative currents of elec-
tricity. No microscope can see them, they are
so small; but men in laboratories play with
them, divide them, unite them. There is as big
a world down through the microscope as there
is up through the telescope. God made it all.
The more mysterious and incomprehensible this
vast creation becomes, the more sure grow the
scientists that a great Mind lies behind it, created it, presides over it, and directs it to a purpose of his own. I need not follow the trains
of thought of these great physicists, like Ed-
dington, Haldane, Jeans, Pupin, Millikan.
Enough for me to assure you that the leading
scientific minds of to-day tend strongly away
from the nineteenth-century mechanical view of
creation toward a distinctly theistic conception.

The trouble with us ordinary mortals just
now is that we have lost our six-foot God and
have not grown up to our light-year God, the
God of the galaxies and the God of the atoms.
Our minds reel and stagger before his strange
and mighty works. They reeled and staggered
before, when we looked up into the sky with un-
aided eyes and saw the myriad stars. Now that

creased. Competition, ruthless and inhuman, has grown apace. The few, always inclined to ride over the many, have ridden more selfishly and more destructively by means of the inventions of our scientific era, until millions have been thrown out of work, thousands appear in breadlines, and hundreds of families starve and freeze, while hundreds of others suffer on the rack of uncertainty and unhappiness. Business men look careworn. Extra lines come into their faces and white hairs multiply upon their brows. We don't know what's the matter with us. The trouble is we have lost our six-foot God and we have no other to take his place. We shall find him; we are finding him; we shall never rest content until we have laid hold upon him. As the hart pants for the water brook, the dryer and harder the times, so humanity pants for God and can never rest content until it finds him.

The grown-up God, the scientific God, the God of the modern time, must be a God of law. He can never keep these galaxies, weighing millions of millions of millions of tons, swirling like puffs of smoke in space without law, rigid, regular, implacable, and irrevocable law. We all live under law and die under law. Let us get that through our heads and quit talking that "God in his infinite mercy has taken out of this body the spirit that inhabited it." God's infinite mercy had nothing to do with the cancer, or the typhoid, or the pneumonia that took out of this body the spirit that inhabited it. God's infinite mercy had nothing to do with the death of young Sheridan, the West Point cadet, in a football game. Sheridan broke his neck, that's all, as he charged against the stone wall of the law. No use asking God to put his fingers into the creation and stop the operation of the law. One of those galaxies might swing out of its place if he interfered even in the life of one single man, and the whole thing might go to wreck and ruin. No, he will not change the law. It will go on just as relentlessly as the worlds swinging through their orbits.

This new God, however, must be a beneficent God. The law that he created must operate forever for the good of the minutest creature upon the minutest speck of dust which we can call a world. With every breath you and I draw, millions of those molecules pound like rifle bullets upon the inside of our lungs and act just like the steam upon the piston, to keep us living, breathing, moving, speaking, and singing. How wonderfully good, then, is this law of our new and more majestic God. "The will of God," which we now call law, is all for us and never against us, for our welfare, for our safety, for our growth. Ours to find out as nearly as we can what the law is and live in harmony with it.

Moreover, this mighty God is a God of intelligence. The more we know of his vast creation, the more we respect that high intelligence. Ours to meet him with as great intelligence as we can summon. Wrongdoing, then, becomes unintelligent conduct. The wicked thing is to attempt the impossible. Our ethics finds its ground in the orderliness, the perfection, of the law.

Once again, this tremendous God stands all round us, over us, beneath us, inside of us. We are compassed about by the reality of his presence, his help, and his strength. No man need be lonely who turns his heart outward to meet the realities with which he has enshrouded us. Closer is he than breathing, nearer than hands and feet.

But I want to see him, cries the impatient soul. I want something more concrete than you have given us. You have merely staggered my mind with the greatness of the picture you have tried to draw. Very well, then, see him in the yellow and the scarlet of the maples, the oaks, and the sumac. See him in the clouds and the sunshine. See him in the beauty of a baby's face, in the stumbling prattle of a baby's voice, and in the sound of running water. Everything beautiful presents the concrete picture of your God. And see him in the truth, the truth that these astronomers send out from Mount Wilson and the patient men who tell us what is under their microscopes. See him in the truth that daring men speak and write and pass on to us. See him in the truth that shatters even our old foundations and makes us, whether we will or no, build new ones. Whatever else fails, our devotion to truth we must never let fail. Truth may be tragic, but always it is beautiful. Oftentimes the most beautiful poetry, painting, living, may be most tragic.

Then see him in the good. Whatever of satisfaction comes to us, whatever of happiness, believe that it comes from God and see that it is a reflection of his ordering mind. Whatever fine and noble you behold in any other human being, that is an attribute, yes, a mirror of our new and majestic God. Have you seen any man or woman doing a thing of which your mind and heart with a certain enthusiasm approved? Then that is a flash from God. Anything heroic, anything courageous, anything ploddingly persevering and doggedly determined, any holding on like grim death to a purpose and a plan —any such manifestation in a human being presents a picture of the eternal Creator. That is God in action in a human life. What a piece of work is a man!

For millions of us in this Western world, which has brought most of our science to light, the picture of God appears to us in the face and

figure of Jesus who was called the Christ. He
gathers up into himself, as no other human being has ever done, the true, the beautiful, and
the good. When, therefore, we would read of
God in the book that we can all best understand,
we turn to the book called Christ. Whenever
we find it impossible not to pray, we call out
upon our God and immediately there arises before our eyes the face of the Nazarene. That
man will never lie to us; he will never cheat us;
he will never mislead or deceive. He is the
truth embodied; and if we but listen to him, he
will give us just that truth that we need.
Search through his words and see.

If anyone does not know what to believe, let
him turn to the words of Christ and ponder over
them. He will find what to believe. If anyone
hesitates about a course of conduct, let him
listen to the word of Jesus from the mountain
top and he will find his doubts resolved. If anyone is hungry-hearted and lonely, or suffering
in body or in mind, let him listen to the con-
soling Christ and he will find companionship,
help, peace, and strength. If anyone finds himself hard put to it to make both ends meet in
these difficult days, let him walk with the Nazarene over the hills of Judea or in the valleys of
Galilee, and catch his spirit as he walks and
talks; and that one may or may not find increase
of this world's goods or added security in his

job, but certainly will find a sense of peace that none of these things can give and none of them can take away.

Nowhere else in human life can the beauty be found that is found in him. Some pastoral beauty, some social beauty, some poetic beauty, then at the end great tragic beauty. Yes, no such beauty has ever been spread before human eyes as the supreme beauty in the life, the death, and the continuing power of that young man of Nazareth. Surely if God is anywhere in human life—and he is everywhere—then preëminently is he there in Christ. And goodness? Every human being recognizes his goodness. As the conscious water saw its God and blushed, so does humanity, whenever it looks upon the face of Christ, cry out in adoration of his goodness as contrasted with its own frailty. To see Jesus with the eye of faith and imagination is about as near as any of us can come to seeing that more than six-foot God.

III

IS GOD LOVE?

God is love. 1 JOHN 4: **8.**

THE other day in conversation a friend said to me, "Alexander Procter is the only preacher I have ever heard say, 'God is love.'" I then made up my mind that he was going to hear another preacher say it; but I am going at it in a little different way. There are some listening to me this morning who will be inclined to challenge the bald statement that God is love. They will be hesitant and doubtful because they have gone through deep waters, through the flint-mills, in their lives, or are now in the midst of great difficulties, undergoing pain and distresses, breaking their hearts over disappointed hopes and ambitions, or eating them because of irreparable losses. So I turn the statement round and make a question out of it, "Is God Love?"

In order to think clearly, suppose we ask the preliminary question, "What do you mean by God?" That is a very real inquiry in our time; and perhaps there are not a great many of us who are entirely certain just what we do mean by the term. A surprisingly large number of

30

us have never got away from our childhood conception of him, that he is a big man with a gray beard and a mighty, powerful arm, sitting somewhere localized in space, out yonder to the east, or more likely up yonder overhead, that he smiles and frowns according to the weather and that he rewards or punishes according to whether we are good or bad. It is very difficult, even for most thoughtful people, to get away from that naive childlike conception. You would be surprised to know, doubtless, how many Church leaders think in terms of that kind.

Now, this age of ours, perhaps it is safe to say, is more aware of the existence of a personal power back of our world and of our life than any other age has ever been. Our scientists and our philosophers are theists in greater numbers than intellectual leaders and learned men have ever been in history. The old mechanical view of this frame of things that so many scientists used to hold does not stand up under modern discoveries. The notion that this world and all the worlds is just a huge machine that set itself going and keeps itself going, without any soul in it, or any person back of it, becomes increasingly untenable. The thought that matter is the beginning and the end of it all, that we ourselves are matter, muscle, and nerve, with a piece of meat for brain and heart,

and altogether our whole life is the result of the
action of certain glands that are subject to no
personal creative power outside of us, that we
came from dust and shall return to dust, dying
as leaves die or as dogs die, is a theory that
does not answer. In fact, we are beginning to
see that even matter itself is too complicated
simply to be called matter, that the atom of so-
called matter is itself a compound particle made
up of what we are now calling electrons, the elements of force, positive and negative poles of
that something which we have long called elec-
tricity or magnetism, that power that thrills and
throbs through all the structure of these complicated worlds. So matter is not the end-all and
be-all; there is force, mysterious, inexplicable,
coming from somewhere and going somewhere.
What shall we call all that sum of force, that is
so beautifully harmonious, so grandly persistent, so nobly directed toward some apparent
aim? Most of us have no other word for it except God. It, or He, cannot be located, defined,
circumscribed. He has no dwelling place, no
throne, no fixed habitation or limitation,

> "Whose dwelling is the light of setting suns,
>   And the round ocean, and the living air,
>   And the blue sky, and in the mind of man."

This force, this power, this personality, this
God, of whom we are all a part, in whom we

First, then, life is good; it is a boon to be alive at all. Here is one good gift that the Great Power has bestowed with a regal prodigality. He has sown conscious life broadcast through at least this one world with a magnificent extravagance. And with what joy is the mere possession of life accompanied! All the sorrows and all the pains and the absolute certainty of inevitable death cannot rob a living creature of the inexpressible happiness to be found in just being alive. Every spring up to two years ago, a pair of mocking birds built their nest and reared their young in a huge old walnut tree that shades our sleeping porch. At daylight every morning the daddy-bird, on one of the highest twigs, with just enough leaves above him to hide him from eyes that might be dangerous, would lift his little head and swell his melodious throat in such a song of conscious joy as few creatures on earth except himself can sing. And all through the night one of the little fellows, the eldest son, I imagine, in the nest used to wake up and practice, about once an hour I should judge, against the day when he too should stand on a topmost twig and sing out his joy in living and in fatherhood. That little fellow would make many false starts, and go back and begin over again, with infinite patience and pains. With all the assiduity of an expectant prima donna he would tune up his

God-given little instrument and seek a masterly
control of his wonderful little vocal chords.
Then it seemed as if he would grow drowsy, and
his tones would become less and less controlled,
until finally he would drop off into the silence of
sleep. In another hour or so he would wake up
and go at it again. Is it a good power, a kindly
God, that gave that little fellow his joy of living
and of singing? The two-year-old child learning to manipulate hands and feet, spending
hours running up and down, doing this and that,
is occupied in precisely the way that the little
songster so thrillingly enjoys. It is the happiness of existence and of increasing skill.

The world is bristling with that joy, over-
crowded with it. This springtime I have been
out to many commencements and made many
journeys across four or five States. I have seen
beautiful and wonderful things. What luxuri-
ant life the summer has spread all over the surface of the earth—blue grass knee-high to feed
myriads of living things; wheat waist-high and
ready to be cut; the woods heavy with foliage,
deep and shadowy sanctuaries for myriads of
feathered and furry creatures possessed of the
wondrous joy of living; the streams clear and
cold, dashing and still, the homes of sentient
beings in swarms—life everywhere, abundant,
rich, and beautiful life! Surely it is a Good
Power that gives it all.

I know the drawbacks—few better—the troubles, the sufferings, the pain of body and of mind, the losses, disappointments, disillusionments, and tragedies. I am well aware of these in my own life and in the families of you who listen to me to-day. I see it all the time and feel it all the time, and yet I see, I think, unending triumphs over these very drawbacks and handicaps and sufferings. Every one of us has seen some lives that were all the more beautiful and radiant for drawbacks that we outsiders would think insuperable. That is a common sight and these are trite words.

What I am most anxious to say is this: that all kinds of drawbacks and handicaps are more powerful in the imagination than in the reality, that it is the mind which suffers so much more than the body ever does or ever will have to, that it is fear and dread of anticipated ill which causes more actual pain than anything else in human life, and that perhaps the good God intends that a time may come when we shall conquer this most potent source of human woe and rise far superior to it. We have only just begun to try, and perhaps what we call misfortune and suffering were put here as a challenge to exert our hitherto unused powers. I know we cannot solve the problem of evil, but may this idea not be an element in the ultimate solution, the idea that evil is here as a grindstone on which to sharpen our blade, that it is here as a dummy for us to tackle in the way football candidates tackle a straw man cased in leather, that it is here as the north wind and the storm are here for us to breast, to overcome in order to develop our lungs. Fear is the concentrated evil, the personification of ill; and if we can once think of fear as a being that we are to fight with and to whip and to knock out, may it not help us to an understanding of our Creator who put us here amid fears?

So many of the boys overseas were terribly smitten with fear. The man who says he was not afraid under fire is either a moron or a liar. All of them were afraid; oftentimes the most intelligent and most sensitive were the most afraid. Then many of them mastered fear in most unexpected fashion. Sir W. Beach Thomas, in the *Atlantic Monthly,* tells of a British boy who frankly confessed to his over-powering fear in the trenches. His corporal told the captain that that boy would some day desert, or that they would have to shoot him for trying to run away, as many a soldier was shot by his own officers. The boy meditated suicide, thought of giving himself up as a prisoner; and one night he could stand it no longer and crawled out of the trench into no man's land to go across to the enemy and give himself up. He became confused and wandered about for hours in that desolate and dangerous country. Then just at dawn he came suddenly slap-bang up against a machine gun, and he heard low guttural voices and saw the machine gun swinging round with muzzle toward him. Then he knew nothing more until he found himself in a narrow dugout under a board with two dead Germans at his feet, and he knew he had killed them. Cutting off their insignia, he shouldered the machine gun and made his way proudly back to his own trenches with his trophies. They put him in the hospital for a few weeks on account of a gash in the calf of his leg and other minor injuries. He could scarcely bear the time of waiting until he should get back again into the lines to exercise his new-found courage, the bravery he possessed, of which he had not dreamed.

So many of us—yes, all of us—could be rid of fear, if only we would make up our minds to assert our unknown heroism. Why be dominated in all our living by a thing we know to be imaginary, a mere figment, a mere superstition? Let's walk out of here braver, let's be afraid of no man and no circumstance, no disease and no pain, no death itself; for it is not half so fearful—whatever it is—as we anticipate it to be. That power which gives the pain administers also the opiate and in the hour of death the anæsthetic. It looks to me as if that power is kindly, beneficent, and that God is love.

It is time for us to turn now to that Thinker who knew more about God than any of the rest of us have ever known or will ever know, and to ask him what he thinks about it. What does Jesus say? We accept his words in everything else in our lives and try to put them into practice. We never question his wisdom, his judgment, and his sanity in all our social, ethical, and even legal relations. Should we not give weight to his opinion in so intricate and so profound a matter as this question, What kind of God have we? He says God is love. He says God is a Father. Fatherhood and motherhood are the other names for love. The rare exceptions only prove the rule. Some few of you think you had bad fathers; and fewer still will agree your mothers were bad—but so very, very few; nearly everybody considers his father and his mother the ideal of what parenthood ought to be. This mere fact proves that fatherhood and motherhood have been pretty successful in convincing human offspring that they are the other name for love. Now, Jesus called God Father and urges us to call him father. He describes him as exercising even a maternal care over all his creatures from the sparrow to the sheep, from the flowers to human beings.

Jesus uses every figure and every illustration

that his unmatched literary skill can produce in a struggle to convince an apparently reluctant humanity that God's chief characteristic is not power so much as love. He tells us how the shepherd folding his sheep at night, a hundred of them, the most helpless and the most timid of all four-footed things, counts them and even calls them by name, and missing one of them goes out on a search in the night, in the storm, on the mountain, until he finds that one. And lifting it to his shoulder he carries it home. God is love. He tells us of a father who has two sons, and one of them begs for his share of the property, and, taking it, goes and squanders it in the gambling dens and hell holes of distant cities, then comes home penniless, ragged, and hungry. The father sees him a long way off, and going to meet him throws his arms about the filthy wreck of humanity and with tears takes him to his heart. The so-called story of the prodigal son ought not to be called that; it is really the story of father-love. God is love.

Over and over Jesus tries to picture that love, the love of God. Think over his words, and can you recall much that he said about the power of God? He does not emphasize God's omnipotence, nor even his omniscience. Never once does he say, "God is vengeance, God is wrath, God is retribution, God is everlasting punishment." On the contrary his whole emphasis is upon the tenderness, the kindness, the gentleness, the protection, the love of God. I know what a hard time he had to convince the people who listened to him, and how hard a time he has even now to convince us of the love of God. I know what a hard time we have to comprehend that love, to picture it to ourselves at all, indeed to picture God to ourselves at all. It is an almost utter impossibility for our little minds, our childish imaginations, our limited and restricted power. Who can form any adequate notion of the Almighty?

Well, here is another way we can get help in trying to figure out what God is like. He is like Christ. Can you imagine Christ? Surely you can. The picture may be inadequate; so is your mental picture of Washington, of Lincoln; but some picture of both these men and of all great historical characters whom you have never seen you undoubtedly all have. We do not all have the same picture of Christ, but for the matter of that we don't have the same picture of anybody alive or dead or anything on earth that ever has been or ever is. That's one of the beautiful things about life, that we are all so different, so individual, so diverse. No matter what our powers of imagination, then, or our limits, Jesus, recognizing our difficulty, told us in so many words that if we wanted to make a picture of God to satisfy our minds and hearts, just to think about him and to picture him. He said, "I and my Father are one. I do always the things that please my Father." And when Philip said to him, "Show us the Father," he answered, "Have I been so long time with you, and yet have you not known me? When anybody sees me he sees the Father. So how can you say then, Show us the Father?"

I imagine, too, that most of us, when we try to make a picture of God, do see the face of Christ rising before us. It may be shadowy and ill-defined, or it may be clear-cut and plain, according to whether we have read and thought a great deal about him or whether we have not. Anyway, I imagine that most of us, when we pray, pray not so much to God as to Christ; in our prayer the face of Christ comes before us inevitably and persistently, for he is the only picture of God we have. And certainly Jesus himself is concentrated love. He is the essence of love. He is the personification of love. Greater love has no man than he. No such love has any man as he had and has.

So our question is answered, "God is love." Our age, which is a God-hungry age, seeking him who is the mysterious power back of all our science, all our discoveries and our triumphs, that strange and beautiful power which we see manifested in all force, and in all matter which we have now found out to be force, we find to be beneficent. The boon of life which is given us is almost entirely good, and the best is yet to be because we are beginning to understand that even the shadows and the defects and the somberness of life are due to our own foolish fear, our over-vivid imagination. Believing, then, that God is good and that nothing can befall us under his charge, who is so mindful of his own, and taking the word of Christ at its face-value that this great power back of all is personal and is nothing less than a father in his love for us, why should we not go on our way with heightened courage, with increased joy, to live and not fear, and to trust that Father who is so like our Christ?

THE MAN WHO PLAYED GOD

Not a sparrow falls to the ground without your
heavenly Father.   MATTHEW 10: 29.

NOT long ago I saw George Arliss in a pre-
view of a talking picture called "The Man Who
Played God," made from the story with the
same title by Gouverneur Morris. The picture,
due no doubt to the consummate art of Mr.
Arliss, made a profounder impression upon me
than did the written story. I think most of the
audience, like myself, shed many tears.

A great American musician, a pianist, takes
Paris by storm. Everybody who is anybody
has heard him play; and although he is a man
of advancing years, all the young women of the
French capital adore him, follow him about in
the streets and hotel lobbies, and ask for his
autograph. A young American girl, his pupil,
goes about with him and tries to shield him
from the pursuing multitudes. His sister
serves as his secretary. He disclaims that he is
a genius, declares that eight hours a day of
hard work for twenty years has brought him his
skill, and refers to his mother who, it develops,
went stone deaf while still in middle life. Re-

vealing a deep religious nature, he examines in his suite in a Paris hotel the photograph of an organ which he intends to donate, in memory of his mother, to the little old home church in America.

He is to give one final concert before leaving for home and informs his close friends that he is to play at this concert for a king who is to be present incognito. His pupil, a charming young American girl, left alone with him, avows her love for him. He considerately and tenderly repulses her, telling her he is old enough to be her grandfather, at least her father. She declares that this makes no difference to her, and he finally agrees that at the end of six months, if she feels the same, he will marry her.

That night the king is delayed by a motor accident, but comes in just as the concert is over. Then the great musician sits down to play for him at the piano in the reception room behind the scenes in the theater. Some enemies of the king, trying to assassinate him, throw a bomb into the place. The king, unaffected, coolly tells the great master to go on with his playing. The latter tries to do so, but finds that he has gone stone deaf.

Returning to New York, the musician, his sister, and his valet, a faithful body servant of many years, are all plunged into the deepest

despair. For five months the musician will see
nobody. In gloom and rebellion he keeps his
room. Finally he admits to his presence his
young girl pupil, who writes down on a pad
whatever she has to say to him until, distressed
beyond endurance, he drives her away. Then
comes an old friend, Mildred, perhaps a sweetheart of the long ago, and to her he unburdens
himself of his despair. He opens the Bible and
reads to her about the two sparrows which sell
for a farthing, and yet not one of them falls to
the ground without the Heavenly Father. He
declares bitterly, "I no longer believe in your
God. He is a cruel God. He has taken away
the one thing I loved in life, my music; and I
hate him!" One day he tries to leap out of his
high window to death and is restrained by his
body servant. The physician suggests to his
sister that they should give him lessons in lip
reading. Finally they gained his reluctant consent, and employed for him the best teacher.
In a remarkably short time he becomes a master
of the art so that he can see what people are
saying with perfect ease.

One day, taking up a pair of field glasses, he
looks down into Central Park. He can watch
people talking to each other on the benches
there and know all they say. He sees a young
man, scarcely able to walk, talking with his
fiancée. The doctor has told the boy that if he

keeps on working in the city he will die of con-
sumption. It will cost at least a thousand dollars for him to go out West. The young people
are in despair. The young man begins to pray,
only his lips moving. Arliss turns from the
window, shouts for his valet and sends him hot-
foot down to the park to obtain the name and
address of the young man and to assure him
that God is going to answer his prayer and will
send him the money.

From this on he watches daily from his window all the problems of the people who pass up
and down in Central Park, the needs of the little
children for toys, the distresses and the sorrows of many in despair, and through his man
he ministers to the needs of these passers-by
in his life. He becomes a changed man as he
thus plays God, anonymously, for those who
come and go before his eyes. Finally his young
girl pupil, who has now fallen in love with a boy
of her own age, comes back to fulfill her prom-
ise. She, too, takes a seat on a park bench to
bid good-by to her young lover before entering
the apartment to give herself in marriage to the
older man. He reads her lips, although Mildred tries to take the glasses out of his hands.
He learns the truth, and when the young girl
appears he renounces her and sends her away
to her boy. Then for the first time since misfortune came he turns to his piano. Once more

he looks at the photograph of the organ, which
has now been installed in the church, and finally
agrees to be the first to play it. In the last
scene, the woman friend goes with him to the
empty church. He sits down at the console, and
with just the two of them present he begins to
play "Onward, Christian Soldiers."

These words of mine only haltingly tell this
story, and can give nothing of the impression
borne in upon the heart by the vividness of the
picture and the superb acting of Mr. Arliss.
There is a great sermon in that picture. Four
stages of human experience after the coming
of his great affliction: desolation, substitution,
adaptation, and revelation.

First, comes the utmost desolation and even
desperation. The most precious thing in a
man's life suddenly wrenched from him, the loss
drives him to the brink of self-destruction.
First or last, most people encounter in their
experience such a period. Rebellion sweeps
their hearts like a storm. They see the cruelties
of nature and of the law; they cannot believe
that a good God could permit the accidents that
happen in the world, the pain and suffering,
the deprivation and the losses. Anyone who
has had to submit, ever so reluctantly, to some
physical deformity or inhibition or disease that
cannot be eradicated can understand something
of the rebellion in the heart of this great mu-

sician from whom the very best in his life has been taken away.

After such a time of rebellion, there come to most of us feeble attempts at substitution. We find something to take the place of the old joy, the old freedom, the old power. Some other corners of our minds, even of our bodies, long neglected and left undeveloped, now are rounded out, furnished up, filled with new attractions. Almost nothing is taken away from us in this life but we can find something to take its place. We debate which is the greater affliction, absolute deafness or absolute blindness, or the loss of some member of our bodies or some function, and we can reach no conclusion. We can, however, if we have to submit to any of these afflictions, find a way out, develop something else. Look at the patient blind, look at the patient and inventive deaf, look at the lame and the halt and the deformed. Not one of these but can find a substitute.

Then comes the long and interesting, sometimes inspiring, process of adaptation. It takes skill to adapt oneself to a handicap; and the development of skill always brings joy. One can take what he has left and do with it things that other people cannot do. That in itself confers distinction, creates self-respect, builds up a house within to take the place of the old house that has been wrecked, ruined, even destroyed.

Then can we understand, in a way the prosperous and fortunate cannot do, the true meaning of the hackneyed old poem of "The Chambered Nautilus":

"Build thee more stately mansions, O my soul,
    As the swift seasons roll.
    Leave thy low-vaulted past.
    Let each new temple, nobler than the last,
    Shut thee from heaven with a dome more vast,
    Till thou at length art free,
    Leaving thine outgrown shell by life's unresting sea."

Wonderful the things that handicapped people can do. Armless men write with their toes. Legless men scurry round the streets on little platforms built on casters. Blind men make brooms and get fun out of it, or play musical instruments and derive deep joy from it, write poetry like Milton or compose music like Beethoven. So long as one's head or heart is not destroyed, there remains always something that one can do, and do skillfully and finely, for the good of those round about him and to his own deep and profound satisfaction. One could tell stories by the yard of people so handicapped who have been able to lead useful lives in the world.

Yes, there's the secret of all our loving, whether we are whole or whether we are broken. There lies the revelation—in our usefulness to the society of which we are a part. Once feel useful, once be convinced that one is of some good to somebody else, and life takes on the right flavor. This musician solved his problems by playing the part of a good providence to those crippled lives which hobbled through the park in front of him. He found again that which he had lost, his belief in himself, his belief in the world, and his belief in God. He found it not from any outside authority, a Bible, a church, a person; but he found it by the inner light that irradiated his own darkened soul. So long as he felt useless, so long as he centered his gaze upon his poor self, so long he despaired. When, however, he began to look outward upon the difficulties and dangers of other people and then reached out a hand to help them, then immediately his whole body and soul were flooded with light. That was his moment of revelation; and the light never went out.

There lies the supreme message to you and me of this beautiful work of art from Mr. Arliss. Concentrate our thought and attention upon our little selves, our sufferings and our losses and our deprivations, and the most fortunate of us cannot some day escape despair. Life does not hold unalloyed happiness for any whose attention is centered upon themselves. No wonder Jeanne Eagles in "Rain" could say, as the curtain went down on the last act, "I am sorry for everybody." All the little world she lived in, the only world she knew, seemed the world of egoism made up of little self-centered beings. And since most of us form for ourselves the center of the universe, one can well say of nearly everybody, "I am sorry for everybody." What a series of jams human life is. How it hinges upon the things round us, the health and well-being, the possessions and the ease. When these are taken away from us, how natural and how easy to rebel. Take this line of living, and there is nothing for it but to feel sorry for everybody.

Begin, however, to play God for other people, to sharpen the eyes and look for the troubles of other people, and then hurry out to them with help and friendliness, and right away the revelation comes. One begins to believe immediately in those three things that one must believe in, one's self, the world, and God. Here lies revelation. I have got to believe in myself, respect myself; otherwise I land in rebellion and cynicism, where too many of the superficial thinkers of our time have landed and are floundering. Sparrows we are, no doubt, and each of us worth only half a farthing, a coin so small that none of us can conceive it, and yet not one of us falls to the ground, deaf, blind, crippled, broken in body or in spirit, without the knowledge and the care of our Heavenly

Father. That is the revelation. We are of more value than many sparrows.

Neither can we believe in an ordered universe unless this revelation comes to us which lifts us up and out of our little misfortunes and turns our attention to the blind world stumbling on its round of pain. So much evil in the world, or what we call evil. Yes, and so many discords in the great clashing orchestration of Wagner. But out of all those discords and disharmony there comes a mighty avalanche of musical grandeur. Take the individual voices of a great chorus of hundreds of people, and those individual voices may sound like poor broken reeds, off key, without beauty; but taken as a whole they swell into a marvel of harmony and sweet concord. So I think it is with this world of ours, this world of nature, so full of suffering and pain and minor chords, accident and mishap and misfortune, but somehow, in a way we cannot understand because we are not artists enough, making a music noble and vast. That is the revelation. Call it faith if you will, but it is a revelation that cannot come from without, only from within, a sublimated heart.

God himself stands revealed before us when we try to play God. We cannot see him otherwise, cannot measure, cannot define, cannot describe. Far beyond all comprehension, he encircles and enshrouds us. Only when we play providence, begin to serve and help those who limp along the roads of life, can we see him and feel him whom we cannot understand. Then we begin to know that he has walked this world before in many a beautiful life of love and service. Wherever humanity stands up and plays God, immediately God enters in himself. Preëminently in that man of Nazareth, who played God so successfully as to impress upon the world his godlikeness, do we see the face of that Heavenly Father who marks the sparrow's fall. Even in our desperations, then, we may find a substitution for our losses, and adaptation to our broken condition, and a glorious revelation of the supernal beauty in ourselves, in the harmonious world, and in a glorious and kindly God.

I know—not I guess, nor I hope, nor I reason. Our powers of intuition are sometimes far more strong and valuable than our poor powers of reasoning. There are things we know, we don't know how, by a sort of clairvoyance of the soul, a kind of second sight, more clearly and more assuredly than any reasoned conviction. Reason, I sometimes think, of which we are so proud and upon which we vaunt ourselves, is after all a slender staff, at times even a broken reed, to lean upon; while the sight that is within us, given to us we know not how, is so much surer, so much steadier. Time and again I have heard Alexander Procter, perhaps the greatest thinker I ever knew, challenged by some lesser mind in the words, "Mr. Procter, how do you know that? How do you prove that?" His answer was, "I don't prove it. I can't prove it. I just know it." Ralph Waldo Emerson had the same intuitive type of mind. It was not so much a matter of reason with him as a clear-sighted knowledge. He just knew because he knew, and he didn't take time to prove. Call this mysticism, if you will; call it experience, the result of long years of groping and feeling after the truth, the result of wading through deep waters, with storms and tempests raging round your head; call it anything you like, it seems to me far more valuable and a safer foundation under one's feet than all our

little logic, our lame and feeble reasonings.
Reason is not to be despised, but intuition is
greater than reason.

> "Our little systems have their day;
>   They have their day and cease to be:
>   They are but broken lights of thee,
> And thou, O Lord, art more than they!" [1]
>   —Tennyson.

I don't know whether Paul wrote the lines
of my text or not. Many experts think he did
not, but the lines sound to me very much like
him. Anyway, I am sure they were written by
one who had seen what Paul had seen, passed
through what Paul had experienced, known
what Paul had known; and whether they were
written from a dungeon in Rome or not, out of
the stress of the persecution to which all early
Christians were subjected. They are the outgrowth of deep and bitter experience, hardship,
suffering, disappointment, and disillusionment;
and the assurance they convey is worth all that
the writer paid to gain it. "I know!" Maybe
it does take age and the weathering of many a
tempest, the wringing of the heart and even the
breaking of it, to bring that assurance. It is
not an unreasoning assurance, nor an illogical
one. It is just as well supported by reason as
any other conviction upon this subject to which

---

[1] By permission of the Macmillan Company, publishers.

the human mind can come; but it is so much warmer, so much more vital, so much more strong and alive than any fruit of reason can possibly be. Milton, in his blindness, reached the same exalted heights of knowledge and sang of things never before attempted in prose or rhyme.

"Whom," not what. This knowledge is not a knowledge of things, of scientific theories, of theological statements and propositions, of creeds and systems. It is a knowledge of a Person, that great dim, shadowy Somebody who stands behind the world and all this tangled mess and mass of human life, keeping watch above his own; a knowledge of God, that he is, and that he is trying all the time to reach us, as we are so hungry to reach him. More than that, it is a knowledge of his Son, his picture of himself, his portrait given to us in the Man of Nazareth, Son of Man and Son of God. The old prisoner in the dungeon cell of this world does not need proof, does not have to demonstrate that God is and that his Son is like him. He knows it *de profundis,* out of the depths. He has experienced contact with the unseen Father of us all and with his Son, the Man of Sorrows whom he has sent to show us what he is. "I know whom." How can I dispute any more over little teachings about him, about definitions, about the divine in him or the deity

in him; about the church he never built, about
the entrance into it which he never prescribed,
and the tests of fellowship he never defined?
I cannot dispute at all. All dispute falls to the
ground beneath the immensity of this profound
knowledge, this deep assurance, "I know whom
I have believed."

"I have believed." Yes, that was in the
past, before all the deep waters and the heavy
scourging had fallen upon the lone prisoner in
the dungeon at Rome. There was a time when
the best he could say was, "I believe." That
time is not to be despised. It is part of the
aging process of the soul; it is the day of childhood in Christ, when milk and not strong meat
was our fare. Then we believed, then we had
hope, then we earnestly desired, and perhaps
the wish was father to the thought. In those
days we sought proofs and demonstrations; we
tried to reason our way through to the conviction that there is a God, that we are kin to him,
and that he pays some attention to our little
lives. But that day fades and passes, and with
its passing comes the unshakable conviction,
the knowledge beyond all peradventure of
doubt; and we graduate from the little school
of "I believe" into the great free air of "I know
whom." It is not for us to despise the day of
"I believe." It is the beginning for us all, and
is far better than the age of "I do not believe."

It is at least the entrance to the path that leads, it may be through thick wood and deep valley, across swollen streams and the harsh hillsides of experience, up to the clear summit of the mountain top where we can say "I know." "I believe" is the stage at which all of us who try to be Christians or religious people at all have started and must start. It is the stage of faith which practically all who listen to debates now occupy. If all would declare even so much, it would help them immeasurably on the rest of the journey to the high summit of "I know."

"And am persuaded." That means, "I am convinced," by argumentation perhaps, more likely by hard knocks. There are various ways of persuading an animal, a child, or a man. Reason persuades, logic persuades, instruction and the lash persuade, gentle and kind words and guidance persuade; in short, life, with all its experiences, its hopes and fears and punishments, persuades or leads us to our final convictions. To be fully persuaded, then, is to be able to say, "I know." That word "persuaded" sounds like Paul to me, for it was a favorite word of his. In his highest and most triumphant flight of eloquence, he cries out to the Church at Rome, "I am persuaded, that neither death, nor life, nor angels, nor principalities, nor powers, nor things present, nor things to come, nor height, nor depth, nor any other creature, shall be able to separate us from the love of God, which is in Christ Jesus our Lord.'' That is the same persuasion or conviction or certainty that is expressed in our text. It is assurance of God, of his love, of our inalienable relationship to him, of our unending immortality. Paul not merely believes all these things, but he knows them; and I do not hesitate to say that the greatest minds and souls in all times and nations, under all ages and all religions, have for the most part—if not early in life, then late in its experiences—reached the same bedrock of certainty. This great cloud of believers, yes, of knowers, ought to add to our own assurance.

''That he is able.'' Of course we know he is able. Look at all his power that swings these worlds through their orbits, that causes life to bud and burgeon through a thousand and ten thousand springs and summers, that leads every life through a complicated labyrinthine pattern with a definite purpose to a final goal! To be sure, he is able. All power is his. He can make and mar and in countless ways alter and change and reshape the face of the world and the destiny of a human life. It takes little to persuade us of the ability and the power in that great hand and arm. A storm on the ocean, a cyclone on the plains, the bowing of oaks and elms beneath the lightning and the wind, the roaring heat of summer on western deserts, the plunging of a mighty, tawny, turgid river, uprooting trees and carrying away houses in its resistless motion toward the sea—you have but to look around you to see the manifestations of his resistless might. The hard thing for humanity is to come to know that all that power is beneficent and kindly, directed toward good ends, just as good ends as the material with which it works enables it to achieve. This is part of the conviction, the intuition, the mystic knowledge, that comes out from that cell at Rome and from the dungeon in which dwells many a human heart.

"To keep that which I have committed." Everything is committed to his keeping—hopes and aspirations, loves and losses, heartbreaks and disappointments, mistakes and failures, all the thousand and one little things so precious to the heart of man. All these we have committed to his keeping. The graves of our fathers and our mothers, the little mound under which lies the dear child loved long since and lost awhile, the frustrated ambitions of broken and truncated lives, the disappointments in those whom we had trusted, and the disillusionments about the fineness of humanity and our expectations of what it would do and be in the greatest emergencies that confront it. Anything, everything, that concerns us most deeply, we have committed to him, for we are helpless to handle them for ourselves; and he holds them as in the hollow of his hand. He is able to keep them, and he will keep them. Is it a child whom we cannot manage, a head-strong son or daughter, he is able to know them and he will keep them. We cannot live their lives for them; it is all we can do to live our own. Remember the Master's picture of the shepherd who carried the lost sheep in his arms. Remember how Jesus himself followed up the lost, strayed, and stolen, how little time he had for the safe, the conventionally good, the right-eous of his day. He had all the time in the world for those very ones who seemed to be lost in the thickets of this world. What he was and what he did, that his Father is and his Father does. He is able to keep that which we are not able to keep. Is it a deferred or a frus-trated hope of our own heart that eludes us and leads us on with hungry heart through in-creasing days and advancing years? He keeps that, too. Mere hope may be the best thing in the world for you and me—better than the reali-zation. The yearning, the reaching, the stretch-ing on may be deepening the soil of our souls or touching the muscles and sinews of our be-ings. We know that he is able to keep it, to cherish it, to give it life and not to let it die, and maybe in the end to bring it to realization

in a far finer and better way than we can now
see and understand. It was so when Jesus told
his twelve apostles that they could not follow
him then to the cross, to death, they were not
ready; but they should follow him in the long
run when they were ready.

"Against that day." What day? Any day.
To-morrow, next year, the day of the great im-
pending tragedy or the day of unexpected relief
and release that may come into our lives, the
day of death, the day of judgment, whatever
day the future may hold for any of us. There
are days of plenty waiting for us, days of trial,
of storm and stress, of peace and beauty, of radiance and joy, transition days when we pass
over from one stage of what we call this life to
another and a larger stage of what we may call
another life. It is no odds what that day may
be nor when it may come. He is able to keep
all the issues of our lives against any day and
every day. To be able to face and meet any day
that comes, whatever emergency it contains,
whatever trial or temptation, whatever defeat
or triumph, whatever loss or fulfillment, with
the same calm front and assurance, this is the
outgrowth of the certainty expressed by this old
prisoner at Rome. To live or die is gain. He
is ready to be offered. He would go with equal
calmness to the stake or the cross, or out to free-

dom and to travel in far lands. Whatever the day, it is all the same to him.

Such an assurance as this, that would make us equal to any circumstance or combination of circumstances in our lives, isn't it worth going through fire and water to become ours? What wouldn't we give, any of us, to be able to say with the soldierly assurance of this old traveler of the cross, "I know whom I have believed and am persuaded that he is able to keep that which I have committed unto him against that day"? That heritage may be ours, that assurance may come to us all, that confidence and calm certainty may become part of our nerve and sinew, our blood and bone, the very texture of our souls. I have seen it a thousand times in men and women who, like Paul, have traveled the hard roads of this world. It has seemed that the harder the road the greater the assurance, for beyond the dark pathways, through the thickets and over the rocks, stands the Son of Man and the Son of God waiting in the clear light of the mountain top for those who will keep their breath, draw tighter their belts, and stumble on. He waits as on a mountain of transfiguration to welcome us when we have passed from the shadow lines of faith out into the clear light of certainty.

VI

APRIL FOOL

God hath chosen the foolish things of the world to confound the wise.   1 CORINTHIANS 1: 27.

ALL nations in all times have had one day in the year when they have played practical jokes on their friends, tried to fool each other to the top of their bent, and tried to put each other in some kind of ridiculous hole. The origin of such a fool's day has become lost in the passage of ages. Poor Robin's Almanac one time carried this little jingle:

> "The first of April, some do say,
> Is set apart for All Fools' day;
> But why the people call it so,
> Nor I, nor they themselves, do know."

Perhaps the nearest we can come to accounting for April Fools' day in comparatively modern times comes from the fact that France in 1654 under Charles IX reformed the calendar, making January 1 the beginning of the year instead of April 1 as it had always stood. Many people as usual objected to the innovation; consequently their friends turned the old ceremonies of New Year's day upon these conservatives in a caricatured form, by calling

66

upon them in fantastic dress, by sending them presents which turned out to be cabbages, spoiled eggs, or stones or brickbats, or by playing any other kind of ridiculous prank.

To find a classic origin for All Fools' day we should have to go back to Greece, where a festival to Aphrodite occurred on April 1; and since the constellation Pisces, or the fish, stood in the ascendent at that time, the celebrators chose fish as the appropriate food for this feast. That idea persisted. In France and England only the bravest dared to marry on the first day of April. Napoleon, one of the bravest, did not hesitate to hold his wedding in 1810 to Maria Louisa on that day. Consequently the people of France laughingly spoke of him as "a young fish." Maybe this is the origin of our own slang epithet, "You poor fish."

Anyway, the lesson of All Fools' day stands out clear and plain to you and me, and that is that we are pretty much all fools. Shakespeare could intelligently exclaim, in the language of Puck, "What fools these mortals be!" Old Thomas Carlyle, the cynic, could appropriately refer to the population of England as thirty millions, mostly fools. Were we cynically inclined, we might refer to the population of America in similar terms, one hundred and twenty millions of people, mostly fools. Any one of us who looks back honestly over the

course of his life can point to certain times
when he was an egregious fool. As Tennyson
exclaimed,

> "We are fools and slight;
>   We mock thee when we do not fear:
>   But help thy foolish ones to bear;
>   Help thy vain worlds to bear thy light!"[1]

Deeply consolatory, therefore, this first chapter of Corinthians in which Paul tells us that
"not many wise men after the flesh, not many
mighty, not many noble hath God chosen; but
God hath chosen the foolish things of this world
to confound the wise." The Bible shows us a
great many fools, and does not hesitate to reveal to us their foolish conduct, for which they
always paid and yet in spite of which they often
came out on top. You can pretty nearly call the
roll of the characters in the Old Testament, and
even some of those in the New, and mark their
foolishness. Poor old Noah—he got drunk
just like any other fool. Poor old Samson—he
lost his strength along with his hair because he
confided too much in a woman; literally lost his
head over a woman. Poor old Balaam—he
tried to force his ass to ride over the angel of
the Lord who held a flaming sword in his hand;
and the ass had to turn round and tell him what
a fool he was. Poor old David—he put one of

[1] By permission of the Macmillan Company, publishers.

his best friends, Uriah, in the front line of battle so that he should get killed, and so that David might take his beautiful wife, Bathsheba, away from him, expecting to get happiness out of the transaction. He got nothing but misery. Poor old Jonah refused to go ahead and do his duty and carry God's message where he was told to carry it, with the result that a whale swallowed him up and then regurgitated him on the beach at his destination.

Cross over into the New Testament, and you find a lot of fools. Judas played the fool and paid for it with his life. Simon Peter, the chief apostle, played the fool in pulling out a sword and starting to fight for Jesus, and then played a bigger fool by denying him. The woman who broke the alabaster cruse of precious perfume and mixed it with her tears, poured it over Jesus' feet and wiped them with her long gold hair, what a fool she was; and yet how deathless her fame. The woman of Samaria who went shouting into the town of Sychar, "Come see a man that told me all things I ever did," what a fool she was, because the things she did would scarcely bear the telling; yet what a new light came into her life. Little Zaccheus, the rich tax collector, what a fool he showed himself when he gave up half his goods to feed the poor—the United States government says 15 per cent is enough, and the old Jewish law said 10 per cent

—but Zaccheus has come down through history as a favorite friend of Jesus. Worth it, wasn't it?

> "We are fools and slight;
>   We mock thee when we do not fear:
>   But help thy foolish ones to bear;
>   Help thy vain worlds to bear thy light!" [2]

It would appear from this long list of Biblical characters, and many more besides, that there may be two kinds of foolishness—real, genuine foolishness, and the wisdom that the majority of the world would call foolishness. This latter kind, a foolishness that turns out to be camouflaged wisdom, I think perhaps Paul was talking about when he said that God had chosen the foolish things of the world to confound the wise. "The wise," it would appear in his thinking, means the majority. He shows himself a bit satirical about this majority. Yet here we are in America building our government, staking our happiness and well-being, upon the voice of the majority. We go on the assumption that the voice of the people is the voice of God, that the majority is always right, and that anybody who differs from it should be classed among the foolish. Are we right? Are we wise or are we foolish? St. Paul seems to consider that the majority generally is mistaken, turns out to be

[2] *Ibid.*

unwise and foolish; and watching the drift of public opinion in this free America, this democracy, for the last twenty years or so, one begins to wonder whether or not these words of that wise old lawyer, Paul of Tarsus, may have been addressed not to the inhabitants of old Corinth in Greece but to the United States of America, the population of Missouri and of the city of Kansas City. Could Carlyle say of the people of our city, "Five hundred thousand people, mostly fools"? Could Paul appropriately say, "God hath chosen the foolish ones of your city to confound the wise"?

Channing Pollock has a play called "The Fool." The chief character in this play, a young curate, takes his Christianity so seriously that he gets kicked out of the church, goes into the slums to live, takes the part of the under dog to such an extent that he gets beaten up and sent to jail. What a fool he was! Just a few such fools in the world, who get put into jail for foolish causes, from Paul himself, to Savonarola, to John Bunyan, down to Eugene V. Debs, and yet make themselves immortal. Some modern intellectual has declared that the best a man of independent mind can do in this world is to live with just as much freedom as he can and keep out of jail. A man is a fool who butts his head against the majority to such an extent as to have to go to jail for it; and yet what glorious fellows some of these fools are, God's fools. Yes, undoubtedly Paul must have had in mind two kinds of wisdom, worldly wisdom and eternal wisdom. Which would you rather have?

> "We are fools and slight;
>   We mock thee when we do not fear:
>   But help thy foolish ones to bear;
>   Help thy vain worlds to bear thy light!" [8]

Another very evident lesson comes out of April Fools' day, to the effect that it behooves us all to pass very limited judgments, if any, upon our neighbor's foolishness. We all seem to live in glass houses. Let him that is without foolishness cast the first stone at some other poor fool. Judge not, that ye be not judged. How do we know but that at the very moment we are hurling the stones we may just happen to be in one of our foolish moods or situations. How easy it is to look at the other fellow's conduct and see its foolishness, but be blind to our own. So platitudinous this observation, that nobody seems to think it worth while to guide his conduct by it. We have heard it so often that it no longer tickles our minds into any kind of reaction. Well, then, let's be specific. Maybe concrete instances will do something for us that a platitudinous generalization will fail to do.

[8] *Ibid.*

In hard times it is very easy for us to say,
"Why didn't he save his money when things
were prosperous, so he'd be ready for unem-
ployment and the rainy day? What did he buy
that car for in the first place? He could have
got on without it." Yes, spendthrift foolishness forever walks attendance upon the steps
of us all. You could have seen it in the old
farm homes long before the automobile ever
came along. You could have seen it in the red
plush album on the center table of every farm-
house parlor, yes, the center table with a marble
top. That red plush album, with the cabinet
photographs that used to cost five dollars a
dozen, symbol of extravagance and wasted
earnings—everybody indulged in one. And
how quickly the photographs were dated. Now
we pay five dollars for just one, and who ever
cares anything about them after a few days and
weeks have gone by? I don't want to hurt the
business of the photographers; I am using them
simply as an example of the multiplied extrava-
gances in which we all engage. Perhaps the
momentary pleasure is worth the money. Anyway, the point I am trying to make is that so
long as you have the red plush album, or the
five-dollar photograph of yourself, or the super-
fluous motor car, you have no right to sit in
judgment upon the extravagance of anybody
else. Haven't we all paid too dearly for our

whistles? Haven't we all wasted dollars that now in this moment of depression we would be so glad to have again? If you never have wasted a dollar or a dime, then perhaps you may justly criticize your neighbor for his extravagance.

> "We are fools and slight;
>   We mock thee when we do not fear:
>   But help thy foolish ones to bear;
>   Help thy vain worlds to bear thy light!" [4]

Then, anybody who differs from me politically, religiously, socially, how foolish he is! Why, to a Republican the attitude of mind of a Democrat becomes simply incomprehensible; and to a Democrat it is impossible to understand how a Republican gets that way. Be honest now, you Democrats and Republicans, and own up. Can you understand at all the point of view of a voter in the other party? Well, just at this particular time it would appear to me that you are both fools, that neither party has any wisdom left, that I and a few others are the people and wisdom will die with us. Never, it seems to me, have the two great parties in this country appeared so utterly futile and foolish. They think they are so wise and yet maybe God has chosen the foolish things to confound the wise. Maybe some little minor-

[4] *Ibid.*

ity of foolish ones may some day upset the calculation of both these wise parties. I feel like saying with the fiery Tybalt, after he had been wounded in the fight between the Capulets and the Montagues, "A plague o' both your houses!"

Then, these theological difficulties. What a lot of foolish and loose thinking goes the rounds among the denominations, sects and insects. I can't for the life of me see why the other fellow does not think just as I think. I can't understand why there are three churches in Belton, Mo., which has a population of one thousand people. Seems to me that these three ought to bury their differences and get together in one effective Church. But maybe they are the wise ones and I am the foolish one, though I don't think so. Maybe the old doctrines, three or four centuries old, and indeed forgotten, that divide them, hold a vital importance; but I am just too foolish to see it. Maybe the ladies' aid societies of these three churches get a great deal of spiritual growth out of meeting together, talking about each other, and pulling and hauling the unattached women to try to get them into their particular circles. Maybe that is the wisest possible conduct; but maybe, too, God will choose some foolish one to confound the wise.

Then, socially, how foolish the other person

who does not organize his life in the way that I organize mine. How futile for these middle-aged people to spend nearly every evening playing bridge; and these women to spend nearly every afternoon into the bargain. What fools these young folks be, to go dashing about from night club to night club, or from home to home, or from chicken farm to chicken farm, drinking they know not what. All incomprehensible conduct to me who love conversation and good books. But what right have I to pull to pieces the social ways and manners of my friends and neighbors. Forces stronger than I am, operate upon those lives, whether for wisdom or for foolishness; and we all pass through the foolish phases.

> "We are fools and slight;
>   We mock thee when we do not fear:
>   But help thy foolish ones to bear;
>   Help thy vain worlds to bear thy light!"[5]

We should all like to be wise. In fact, life consists in finding the wise path. We should like to choose the better part, even though it be a minority part, and find our lives glowing and shining with incandescence. I know only one way to accomplish this and change us over on this All Fools' day from absurd thinking and acting to the wisdom that shall confound the

[5] *Ibid.*

pseudo-wise, and that is to get God inside of us, to drink him in and make him part of us, which means to absorb like starving and thirsty people all the true, the beautiful, and the good that we can find round about us in the world of nature in which God reveals himself, in the world of art and literature in which man reaches his highest, and in all the beauty of character which we see reflected in the faces of the most perfect specimens of human beings, the highest revelation of God. If we keep company with his son, Jesus, so calm, so wise, so strong and beautiful, we too may attain to wisdom.

VII

INTERIOR DECORATION

Finally, brethren, whatsoever things are true, whatsoever things are honorable, whatsoever thing are just, whatsoever things are pure, whatsoever things are lovely, whatsoever things are of good report; if there be any virtue, and if there be any praise, think on these things.

PHILIPPIANS 4: 8.

PRACTICALLY all of the great paintings of the world and most of the great sculpture were made for interior decoration. The mural paintings of the capitol at Jefferson City, Mo., cost almost half as much as the erection of the building itself. The frieze of the prophets on the walls of the Public Library at Boston—Amos, Hosea, Isaiah, and the rest—have been copied and are hanging in many homes all over the country. The grandest work of Michelangelo is the ceiling of the Sistine Chapel at Rome. The Last Supper of Leonardo da Vinci on the wall of the refectory at Milan is one of the masterpieces of all time. All these, to say nothing of the stupendous work of Titian in the Doge's Palace at Venice, and thousands of other masterpieces scattered through the world, are intended to decorate interiors. St. Paul, in our text, advises us to spend at least equal

78

care, attention, and artistry on the decoration
of our own interiors.

The art of interior decoration has become a
career in itself. Men and women go to school
in institutes of fine arts and spend years of
preparation to fit themselves for such careers.
They study the proper combination of colors,
harmonies of forms, and lighting systems, and
give their best efforts for a lifetime to making
the inside of homes beautiful, restful, and inspiring. It is an occupation worth anyone's
time and life. Nobody can estimate the amount
of good in quieting nerves, in bringing peace
and content, increasing effectiveness and
longevity, that the interior decorator can accomplish. Great sums are spent and well spent
in making the inside of homes and public buildings just as artistic and meaningful as circumstances will permit. Ought we to spend less
time, thought, and effort on the interior decorations of those houses in which all of us must
live from the cradle to the grave?

The leading thinkers of the world are practically all agreed that living is a fine art, indeed
that the making of life is the finest of all fine
arts. It has to do with the most delicate and the
most subtle of all materials—thoughts, emotions, inward experiences, aspirations, yearnings and longings. To play one's part well, and
to produce a life of the most refined and win-

some quality, is a task to challenge the utmost
ability that any one of us may possess.

> "All the world's a stage,
> And all the men and women merely players.
> They have their exits and their entrances;
> And one man in his time plays many parts."

If a single careless stroke of the mallet upon
the chisel may mar a statue beyond all repair,
so may a single foolish and thoughtless word or
deed injure forever the masterpiece on which
each one of us is engaged. If a single wayward
movement of the brush may lay on colors that
only with great difficulty may be removed, so
may a single slip of tongue or attention damage
the fair painting of our own or another's life on
which we may be engaged. There is no such
sensitive and delicately strung instrument in
all this world as the human heart and soul.
Take heed, then, in playing on it, whether it be
our own or that of another. Hamlet was right
in objecting to the amateurish fashion in which
his false friends tried to play their own tune
on him as if he were a pipe. The art of living
is a nice business and involves not only the
product of a beautiful life for each one of us,
sweet music, good acting, noble sculpture and
painting, but also these same results in the lives
with which we come in contact. No wonder St.
Paul exhorts us to take heed to our interior
decoration.

Not only is active creation involved in the art of living, but also the element of æsthetic appreciation; and this, I think, St. Paul has well in mind. It is not merely what we can and what we cannot create in this world that counts; but it is also what we can appropriate, can understand, can appreciate. Everything in this beautiful world is ours that we can take in and make a part of ourselves. So it is that Jesus could say—and no saying was ever more true—that the meek are the ones who inherit the earth. It is not the man in whose home or in whose gallery hangs the great picture who is the real owner of it; but it is the humble, modest, and all-too-often-forgotten student of the arts who understands that picture at its full value, who is the real owner of it. It is not the man who holds the title deed to the wonderful land of the estates of England, with their beech woodlands, their winding drives lined with poplars, and their historic castles, who is necessarily the owner. The deed may be recorded in the county archives under the name of some sulky and sullen, beef-eating and beer-drinking, fox-hunting and pheasant-shooting, titled nobody who knows nothing of the history and sees nothing of the glorious art by which he is surrounded. Some humble scholar of the middle or lower class, making holidays in this park, may be the real owner. The same may be said of the blue-

twelve million, in one fell swoop, because they didn't know what to do with it when they had got it, except to give it back to the people it came from. That's good, that's fine; more ought to be encouraged to do so. There is nothing any boy can study in high school or in college, there is no book of decency anybody can read, there is no thought or meditation on any legitimate subject—indeed all subjects are legitimate, when rightly used by an artist in living—that does not add to the interior wealth of the thinker. This, I think, is what St. Paul is driving at when he advises us to busy our brain with whatsoever things are true, honorable, just, pure, lovely, and of good report.

Suppose we analyze these six kinds of things, concerning which the old apostle from his prison cell at Rome advises his beloved people at Phillipi, and all the rest of us, to think:

First, he says we should think on whatsoever things are true. True for us, that is to say— things that we know from our own individual experience to be true, things that are a part of us. It is not what somebody tells us that is true for us, certainly not until we have taken it into ourselves, painted it on the walls of our interior, lived it, and made it a part of our very fabric. To read a thing in a newspaper or in a book, to hear a thing said from pulpit or platform, to have it told to us by somebody in conversation, does not make it true for us. It may or it may not be true to somebody else; but we are only concerned in this world with the truth we have made a part of ourselves. The American pragmatic school of philosophy has its limitations; but it got hold of something very vital when it insisted that that is true which works well for each one of us. Each one has his own mural decorations of truth, that belong to him and to no other. He has his own inner niches filled with statuary of his own carving, and nobody has any right to say to him these works of art are not his own. I cannot say to my neighboring minister down the boulevard, "Your system of truth is all wrong and false," just simply because it is not my system of truth. Surely it is his, not mine. Truth is so variable, so many-sided, a gem with so many facets, that there is plenty of its light and beauty to go all round. We shall always differ widely in those phases of it which appeal to us individually. It is the height of foolishness, therefore, for us to quarrel with one another and be intolerant with one another because the pictures hanging on the walls of one are not the same pictures that ornament the walls of another.

Whatsoever things are honorable, these St. Paul advises us to ponder upon. He means things venerable, worthy of honor, hallowed by time, by history, by tradition and association.

He means fathers and mothers. He means sacred old buildings and institutions, historic roads and trails. He means the deeds of our fathers, those lean and level-eyed pioneers, who cordelled their way against the tawny current of the Missouri, two thousand miles, upstream to the Big Horn and the Yellowstone rivers, trading and scouting and fighting, cracking their whips over the heads of long ox-trains on the Santa Fe trail and the Oregon trail, winning a wilderness. He means Philadelphia and Washington, and those men in knee breeches and silver buckles who signed the Constitution. He means the martyrs for truth and right from Stephen and Savonarola to Ridley and Latimer, to Lincoln who died for freedom and unity, to Wilson who died for peace. He means the Church, which for two thousand years has stood and grown against all storms, all corruptions within and without, amid the rise and fall of kingdoms and empires, of races and nations. Go! Think on these things.

Whatsoever things are just. What is fair, what is square, what is even-handed in the relations of man with his fellow man, this is what Paul is talking about. All of us spend plenty of time thinking about our own rights. All of us are jealous enough toward anyone who steps on our toes or into our own little circles of rights. Paul wants us to be equally solicitous about the rights of other people and about keeping our toes out of their circles. We wonder why on crowded streets the other fellow keeps getting in our way. If he is ahead of us, he goes too slow; if he meets us, he ought to be on the other side of the pavement and not get in our way. If we drive a motor car, we are always complaining about the driving of the man in front, or the man meeting or crossing us. We contend that the Fords all get out into the middle of the road and don't give us high-powered people a chance to nose by on the left. We forget that there are higher-powered people than ourselves. Do we know or care anything about how the other half lives? Is it any concern of ours whether they get justice? The men in the shops, in the cattle yards, the janitors of buildings and their hard-bitten families, the children in the mills, old before their time, and dead before they are grown. St. Paul wants us to think on justice for all sorts and conditions of men and women. Only so can we hope to make the interior furnishings of our own houses artistic and beautiful.

Whatsoever things are pure. This embraces nearly everything, for "to the pure all things are pure." God taught Simon Peter by a vision not to call anything common or unclean that had been hallowed by the cleansing of God. To most minds, I know, this word signifies chastity, purity, in just one of the relationships of life. Well, if we cannot get away from that thought, then let us take St. Paul at his word, and think purely, even in this one relationship. God made it. Therefore it is pure in its essence and in its foundation. The American and the English peoples, with few exceptions, are ashamed to discuss this subject candidly; yet I venture the assertion that all who hear me to-day between the ages of ten and fifty spend a great deal of their time consciously or unconsciously pondering the subject of sex. "Hush! Hush! Put on the soft pedal. Don't talk above a whisper"—this is the attitude of the Victorian and Puritan culture under which we are living. How long can we hope to deal adequately with problems arising from one of God's most beautiful means of artistry in any attitude of shame and stealthiness?

We shall never be able to deal with the powerful, poignant, and even painful problems of adolescence until we parents, teachers, and ministers, with open faces and unashamed, deal frankly and honestly with their difficulties. We must begin in very childhood, when every question asked must be answered honestly, truthfully, and without evasion. Otherwise, when it comes time for the next question it will not even be asked for fear of meeting with a lie or hypocrisy. Then the question will get an answer from an undesirable source. This subject is not to be pooh-poohed nor hushed up; God never intended that it should be. St. Paul urges us to think boldly and bravely upon it. Our policy of suppression and repression, of silence, shame, and hypocrisy, has resulted in many neuroses, hysterias, melancholias, and disabilities. It has led to much impurity and crime. The healing work of my Church is overburdened with many who would be wholesome, strong, and well if it were not for our Puritan ancestors and their tradition of hypocritical repression in dealing with this subject.

Whatsoever things are lovely. How much better to ponder upon all the bright and beautiful things in this world and in our experiences than upon the ugly things. Look into your neighbor's face and into his mind and you can see both; but why look at the ugly when the lovely is so much more in evidence? Don't think of enemies when you can think of friends. Everybody that has anything, or is anything, or has done anything, has enemies; but what's the use to think of them? Think of friends, the loveliest gifts of God to men! Don't think of the disagreeable and the bitter things that you hear people say. Think of the sweet and the beautiful things, the brave and courageous and hopeful things. Humanity is only one-tenth ugly; it is nine-tenths lovely. Yet there are those of us who allow the one-tenth to over-shadow, to blot out and to poison, the loveliness of the nine-tenths.

Whatsoever things are of good report. This idea is very closely allied to the loveliness about which the apostle has just been talking. He means the good words, the kind words, the smiling words, the words of praise and appreciation concerning people and things, that we have heard. Turn a deaf ear to evil report, disbelieve it, at least until it is proved beyond all shadow of doubt. Give the benefit of the doubt; listen not to ill fame but to good fame. Look and listen for the harmonious, the musical, the lovely, the artistic. Decorate the interior with harmonious sound and not with discord.

Such are the half-dozen realms of meditation which St. Paul exhorts us to think on. He implies that we can control our thoughts, and we know we can. True, we cannot keep evil thoughts from darting through our brains; but we need not harbor them. You cannot keep the birds from flying over your head; but you can keep them from making nests in your hair. More than that, many a thing, at first ugly and forbidding, may be changed into a thing of beauty and of joy by the alchemy and the artistry of a true follower of Christ. He made everything fair and beautiful that he touched. He took the most unattractive people and transformed them into the disciples and the messengers of his deathless love.

God is doing that all the time. Ariel, the fair spirit, sings in "The Tempest":

> "Full fathom five thy father lies;
>   Of his bones are coral made;
> Those are pearls that were his eyes;
>   Nothing of him that doth fade,
> But doth suffer a sea-change
> Into something rich and strange.
> Sea-nymphs hourly ring his knell."

This song is literally true of the work of God in nature. God makes the wrath of man to praise him. They took his Son and they scourged him till the crimson blood flowed and turned into black under the Syrian sun. They hanged him upon a cross on the hill called "The Place of a Skull." They buried him in the limestone rock, where he suffered some strange change into such newness and such fairness that words have been unable to describe him. We have sought high and low for names and phrases to tell of him; and yet we cannot but feel that all our weak words fail utterly to set forth his truth, his honor, his justice, his purity, his loveliness, and his good fame. When we have nothing else to think of, to save the day for us, and to make our inner life as bright and beautiful as it ought to be, let us think of him.

VIII

NOT WORTH A FARTHING

Are not two sparrows sold for a farthing?
MATTHEW 10: 29.

THE sparrow is the most insignificant of
birds, and the farthing the smallest of coins.
There are Spanish, Italian, and English sparrows. The poor little bird is in every country,
does not migrate, takes the changes of the
season as they come, summer and winter, storm
and sun, and often dies by the thousands in
times of drought and famine. About a hundred
of them would make a pie big enough for one
person. A "fardin" is a quarter of a penny;
and a coin which circulated in Jesus' time,
translated farthing, was about a tenth or a
twelfth of a denarius, the smallest conceivable
legal tender. It took two sparrows to be worth
this little brass bit. Yet Jesus declares that not
one of them falls to the ground without the
thought and knowledge of the Great Creator,
our Heavenly Father. Then he adds, "Are ye
not of much more value than they?"

One time I walked with a companion, just
after a heavy snowstorm, beneath the elms of a
New England city. Paths had been shoveled,

like canyons, through the snow shoulder-high. Suddenly from an ice-coated branch just in front of us something fell to the ground. My companion sprang forward and picked up in his hand a little English sparrow and, blowing his breath upon it and holding it warmly between his palms, tried to revive it, but the little thing was dead. Then he laid it down in the snow and half whispered, "Not a sparrow falleth," while we walked on in silence.

The sailor, tossing in his little craft like a chip upon the limitless mighty sea, feeling his insignificance and helplessness, has taken comfort from these words of Christ and has sung:

> "I know Thou wilt not slight my call,
>   For Thou dost mark the sparrow's fall.
>   And calm and peaceful is my sleep,
>   Rocked in the cradle of the deep."

Really it sounds too good to be true that the mighty God should take knowledge of each individual life in this vast scheme of things. There are so many human beings and there have been so many during the thousands of years that humanity has moved upon this ball. When the pyramids were new, the graveyards of Egypt already teemed with innumerable dead. The banks of the Nile swarmed with the living, soon to be snuffed out. Where now are deserts, then countless millions lived in thriving cities. Great military commanders looked upon their millions of men in arms and wept because they should soon all be gone. Mighty kings before whom multitudes prostrated themselves were swept away like flies in the frost, and we do not even remember their names and habitations.

"The lion and the lizard keep
  The courts where Jamshyd gloried and drank deep.
  And Bahram, that hunter, the wild ass
  Stamps o'er his head and cannot break his sleep."

There are four hundred millions of Chinese and have been doubtless for a hundred thousand years; there are three hundred millions of Hindus and may have been for two hundred thousand years. If you want to be overpowered with numbers of human beings, walk State Street in Chicago, or Broadway in New York, or the Strand in London at busy hours and you will think, where do all these come from, where are they going, and what has become of the countless layers of dead generations over whose heads they move and struggle and fight their way along? Yet Jesus said the Heavenly Father knows every one of them that is or ever has been, and that not one of them has breathed out his little last without the watch-care and the loving attendance of the Great Father of us all. It is just about too good to be believed.

Then, too, how uninteresting most of us are, as drab and brown as the sparrow, that he should take interest in us! What fools are we.

We pride ourselves on the intellect of man and yet how little intellect he has and how little he uses his very small mind. Shakespeare exclaims, "What fools these mortals be!" And shaggy old Carlyle bursts forth many a time, saying something about a nation of so many millions, "mostly fools." What was said then can be appropriately said now. Bring it home and apply it closely to ourselves. We call ourselves in America a nation of rulers of ourselves, that you can't fool all the people all the time, that the voice of the people is the voice of God, that we are a great democracy. All false. We are all fools. We have a few little emotions and we call them thoughts. We don't think with our brains but with our prejudices and deep-seated old conventions born hundreds of years ago. We let our distant ancestry think for us. This is not a democracy, but an oligarchy. We are ruled by a few, rich and powerful men, just a handful, and the so-called statesmen and politicians are only the smoke screen thrown out by these big master minds to conceal their rulership from the multitudes. We talk about electing our own president. Only one-fifth of us even go to the polls; and a little more than half of them, or about one-tenth of the nation, chooses a man, who was chosen in advance for them by the little handful who sit behind the smoke screen and shape our government for us. In the coming election in this State who can vote his convictions? You are shut up to the casting of your suffrage for men who do not represent your thought, who were chosen for you by machines and manipulators, who are the inevitable outgrowth of what we call popular government.

And upon great international questions, who is there of us who uses his brains and does any thinking for himself? Not one in ten million. We think what we are told to think by the manipulators whose labels we wear, by the emotions and prejudices a hundred years old, handed down to us from father to son; and immediately when anybody injects a new thought into the discussion, we cock our wise heads on one side, stiffen our already stiff necks, and refuse to bestir our brains. Thus do nations prepare the way for the deluges that so often sweep away myriads of men. Thus perhaps are we at this very moment preparing the way for the disappearance of white civilization. Very well, maybe it is better so. Maybe the one who marks the sparrow's fall is expecting to see the white sparrow give way to the yellow. We are such fools that it is too good to be true that God should care much about us; but Jesus says he does.

More than that we are so unattractive, so unlovely, so consumed with egoism. We trample over each other as if we were all trying to escape from a fire. We scratch each other and cut each other and hurt each other in a thousand different ways, with hand and tongue, with business and trade, with working conditions and housing conditions and health conditions. It's "Me first and you last." The well-to-do do not care anything about the milk supply of the very poor, so long as they can get good milk for their babies or the babies to whom they choose to play Lady Bountiful. They permit the infant death rate to mount high among the warrens of the poor, because they refuse to think, and only use emotions for thoughts. The exploiters exploit, the profiteers profit, the big business man will not even speak to his employees; what does he care, they are only pawns in his game. Wounded on the battle fields, or stricken down with disease in civil life, and sent to the hospital, what a bundle of concentrated selfishness does almost every patient become! In the ensuing ugliness of illness, how unlovely! Yet Jesus says that in spite of all this our Heavenly Father is aware of every wound and every sickness, he marks the very sparrow's fall.

Human life, so much of it, is drab and dull, uninteresting, monotonous, a deadly boredom. Perhaps that is the spring of much of our un-loveliness. We rejoice in misfortunes, calamities, and crimes because they give us something to talk about and to think about. We snoop and spy on our neighbors and their affairs, which are no business of ours, and gossip about them to break the dull dead monotony of our own empty lives. Or we drink ourselves into insensibility or into a fancied well-being, or we dope ourselves to deaden the pain of emptiness in our little lives. Lloyd George shot a barbed shaft at some suffragettes in his audience one day, when one of them cried out, "If you were my husband I would give you poison." Instantly the little Welshman responded, "If I were your husband I'd take it." Instead of sinking into this slough of boredom, fancy how interesting we could make our modern life. How much joy there is in the complicated concerns of our day! Think of the radio, the motion picture, the vaudeville, the drama, the outdoors, the music, the books—ah, most of all the books—what right has anybody to be bored in this interesting time? We can all read. Yet almost nobody reads. How many business men in America have read a single volume in a year? For that matter, how many women? A few more women, perhaps, but almost none. Yet all these mentally lazy and inert human beings Jesus declared the Good Father loves anyhow, cares for them, and notes every disaster and every decline in their spiritual existence.

Yet, why not? All these creatures are his workmanship; he made us. He is responsible for us. If we believe in a personal God at all, and we all do—we can't get away from that; all the thinkers are agreed that there is a great Power, a great Person, a great Artist, however you care to characterize him, who has made it all and us all—if we believe this, then we must believe that he is interested in all his craftsmanship. Angelo decorating the Sistine Chapel ceiling, or Borglum carving away at a Stone Mountain, must be interested in the smallest line, the minutest surface, the obscurest leaf or cloud of his great design. So the Great Artist, with each of us. There are nearly four thousand people members of this Church; with their relatives, who are not members, there is a company of ten or twelve thousand who regard this Church as their home. I don't know all of them, I can't know all of them; I am not God, and my mind is not infinite like his; but I am interested in everyone of those ten or twelve thousand people, and whatever happens to them, the least of them, concerns me profoundly. So I am sure that Jesus knew what he was talking about when he said that God cared for every one of us. A good physician cannot know all his patients and all their households, but their welfare is his constant thought, by day and by night, and Jesus frequently referred to himself as the

good physician; and what he was, we know God is. He represents God to us, interprets God's thought and character for us. He is the only picture we have of God, and we know that God must be as good as Jesus was.

If all this is true, then, we have the right to place a pretty high estimate on human beings and on every individual human life. With all his defects, his shortcomings, his stupidity, and his unloveliness, man is after all a wonderful little animal. We can't get away from the feeling that he is the center of everything, that all these worlds and constellations revolve about him. We don't know that anybody lives on any of the remainder of these spheres; and whatever our philosophy we all act as if we ourselves were each the center of the universe. So you may not think the life of a coolie, dying on a towpath on the Yangtze River and kicked aside by his companions, amounts to much; but that life is the whole universe to himself and a good part of the universe to some wife or sweetheart or child. One more person knocked down by a motor car, one more child run over, may not seem to count for much as you read of it at the breakfast table; but in somebody's home the whole world is caved in. Every soldier of the thirteen millions killed in the World War was a son of somebody, a husband or a father to somebody whose heart was left desolate. So every life is of untold value to someone else, and Jesus says that every life is just that precious in the sight of the Great Father who made us all.

It follows then that we cannot be too careful of the welfare, not merely the life and the health, but also the growth and development, the happiness and the well-being of every living person.   Our society, our civilization, our boasted democracy, all these are blind and imperfect unless they see to it that every life in them has a fair chance for survival and completion.   Henry Ford seems to be doing his best, according to his lights, to give his people a fair chance, not merely to work but to play and to grow.   Voluntarily he has increased their wages, shortened their hours, and now he has cut off one day from their week of work.   Some of us think he has not seen all the light yet, but he seems to want to see it and to be progressively catching sight of it.   Human beings are not chattels; labor is not a commodity to be bought and sold in the cheapest market.   Labor is made up of human homes, of fatherhood and motherhood, of hope and aspiration, of yearning and loneliness, of comedy, drama, and tragedy.   We have no right to dwarf any life, as, for instance, by making children work in factories before their time.   Life is too precious for that.

It follows, also, from this great value that God places on a human life, that none of us has any right voluntarily to hurt anybody else. Life hurts us all enough. Sometimes duty binds us to perform surgical operations on one another; but never do we have the right to inflict needless pain on those whom our Creator considers of such value that he guards every one of them. On the contrary, sympathy and understanding should be as broad as the world. Not only every little homeless baby in the Near East should successfully appeal for our watch-care, but every citizen in the purlieus of Paris, or among the unemployed in the factory towns of England, every poor half-starved Hindu squatting in the hot sands under the banyan trees of India, every Japanese baby in his little toy house of bamboo, should be of immediate concern to us all. Man's inhumanity to man makes countless thousands mourn, because man is lacking in imagination and therefore in sympathy. You may be sure that God is not lacking in either.

Another result of this estimate which the Creator seems to place upon human life is that, imperfect as we are, he probably intends to give us an opportunity for further development when what we call this life is done. While this is no proof of immortality it is at least an intimation.

IX

AN OLD BRONZE DOOR KNOCKER

Behold, I stand at the door and knock.
REVELATION 3: 20.

THAT knocker is two thousand years old. For that length of time it has either softly tapped or thunderously pounded at the doors of individual hearts or of social structures. It may be called the knocking of the bronze, for bronze stands for dignity as well as antiquity, for artistic beauty as well as for strength. That old bronze door knocker works to-day, ceaseless, persevering, demanding entrance at all doors.

Many knocks come to the doors of apartment houses and even of separate homes these days, so that some of my friends tell me that all day long they would be doing nothing else but open their doors if they responded. This condition of affairs only indicates the complexity, the increasing intricacy, of our social contacts. Perhaps out of twenty who knock upon your door and mine in the course of a day there might be one personality which would bring us an angel's visit if only we opened to him. How is anybody to know? Without a little glass peephole

through which one could look and estimate his
visitors, he has no means of discrimination.
Even if he could look, how is he to know the
angel who may be disguised as an agent or a
collector? Believe it or not, some even of these
are angels. There is something, however, about
this old bronze knocker which makes us aware
most of the time who it is that is tapping at
the doors of our hearts. When Jesus taps,
when his religion knocks, there can be no mis-
taking the reverberation. You and I know who
it is when he taps or thunders at the closed or
half-closed doors of our hearts.

Knock, knock—clamor, clamor—boom, boom!
comes the sound of that old bronze knocker.

Sometimes conscience gives the cue. We
have been doing what we ought not to do and
we know it. We have been leaving undone
what we ought to have done and we know it.
There is no moral health in us because the house
within is divided and we know it. In place of
peace there is conflict. And when the peacemaker comes knocking at the door, when the
good physician stands outside ready to bring us
health and healing, we refuse to let him in because we do not want to undergo the pain of the
treatment or the surgical operation necessary
to our cure. Never mind, he will continue to
knock; there will be no peace for us until we let
him in. So came the knocking of Macduff at

Dunsinane, the castle of Macbeth, in the darkness of the early morning when there was blood upon the hands of the Thane of Cawdor and of his wife, the blood of the aged King Duncan. Knock, knock, knock, came the signal at the castle gates, the signal of the avenger who, before he had done, would bring ruin upon the murderous Macbeth. Nobody could sleep under that knocking except the dead. Macbeth was right about himself when he cried:

> "Methought I heard a voice cry 'Sleep no more!
> Macbeth does murder sleep'—the innocent sleep,
> Sleep that knits up the ravell'd sleave of care,
> The death of each day's life, sore labour's bath,
> Balm of hurt minds, great nature's second course,
> Chief nourisher in life's feast.''

If at the door of our hearts, yours and mine, that relentless pounding comes this day, the knocking of outraged conscience, of failure to live up to our own estimate of ourselves, of unworthiness in our own sight and therefore in the sight of God, it is time for us to open the door and let in the unseen guest, for be assured he will never let us rest nor sleep until we have resolved that inner conflict and have become right with God, which means right with ourselves. We may cry, Peace, peace, but there is no peace. We may long for sleep, sleep, but there is no quiet sleep until we have reconstructed our divided minds, unified our hearts at war with themselves. Forever and forever, throughout the course of our little lives, will come the pounding on our doors:

Knock, knock! Clamor, clamor! Boom, boom!

Sometimes it is opportunity that knocks at the door, opportunity to attain what one long has desired to attain; and then one must answer quickly. Senator John J. Ingalls, of Kansas, made one immortal lyric, on opportunity:

> "Master of human destinies am I!
> Fame, love, and fortune on my footsteps wait.
> Cities and fields I walk; I penetrate
> Deserts and seas remote, and passing by
> Hovel and mart and palace—soon or late
> I knock unbidden once at every gate!
> If sleeping, wake—if feasting, rise, before
> I turn away. It is the hour of fate,
> And they who follow me reach every state
> Mortals desire, and conquer every foe
> Save death; but those who doubt or hesitate,
> Condemned to failure, penury, and woe,
> Seek me in vain, and uselessly implore.
> I answer not, and I return no more!"

That statement is true of many opportunities to grasp what this world calls success. It is not true of the highest opportunity of all, the opportunity to open the door for the Lord of Light. He never ceases to knock, he never turns away, he never fails to give us a second chance, and a third, and endless chances to rebuild and reconstruct and rejuvenate our lives in har-

mony with him and with his word. He stands at
the door and knocks to-day as patiently, as
kindly, and as lovingly as he did nineteen hundred years ago. With gentle insistence, and yet
with penetrating determination, he stands always there, however busied our minds with
other things, and knocks for entrance. It is
for us to let him in. I hear him; you hear him—
however dulled our ears and diverted our attention by the rumble and thunder of this life
and by the patter of voices all round us. We
hear him here at this moment. That's what we
have come here for, to listen to his knocking.
Whether we know it or not, we certainly would
not be here in this place of vantage for listening, if deep down in our hearts we were not
eager to hear. Listen:

*Knock, knock! Clamor, clamor! Boom,
boom!*

Sometimes it is an aspiration, an ideal, a
half-cherished purpose, which he wields as a
knocker upon our hearts. We would like to do
this, we would like to be that, we would like to
achieve the other; but half-heartedly, lacka-
daisically, we have given up, with the lapse of
the years, or we have said, "It is not for me.
It is for somebody else; but I can never achieve
it." Nevertheless, we are not content. We
still cherish the conviction somewhere deep
down in us that even yet we might do it, we

might rise to that height, we might overcome all those obstacles. And even as we think in that way, we have partly opened the door to him; his benignant presence has already come in part way through our stubborn doors; he is already with us, in us, blessing us. To the extent that we still hold our aspirations, still hang on to our ideals, still refuse to be disillusioned completely about life, about our fellows, and about ourselves, to that extent do we still entertain him who forever stands at the door to knock.

He brings with him the solutions to our riddles of existence. Life, so complicated, so intricate, so puzzling, and sometimes even so burdensome, he can solve for us, he does solve for thousands of men and women. Are we perplexed as to how to live? Ask him. Are we eager to know what is the good life? Ask him. He tells us in words so simple that a child can understand him. Listen to his gentle talk on the hillside in Galilee, and then put into use in the practical situations of our daily lives the things he teaches, and we shall find those solutions. Those whom he called blessed are still blessed, the poor in spirit, they that mourn, the meek, the merciful, the pure in heart, the peacemakers, they that are hungry and thirsty for goodness, they that are persecuted and endure hardness for the right—still blessed, thrice blessed. Those that do to others as they would that others should do to them—still blessed. Those that have the courage to meet life, to endure it, to make the most of it, to suffer its hardship and its pain undaunted, the courageous people, the kindly people, the friendly people, they are still the salt of the earth and the light of it. So simple to understand, so difficult to live up to. He knocks at every door of every heart and calls on every one of us to undertake this most difficult adventure in the world, the most delicate and skillful undertaking to which men have ever set their hands, the living of the good life. You can hear his voice to-day saying again, "Behold, I stand at the door and knock."

Knock, knock! Clamor, clamor! Boom, boom!

These days his knocking has grown into a thunder in the world. To-day he stands at the door of stock exchanges, of departments of state, of executive mansions and the palaces of rulers. He is pounding upon the seats of empire and hammering at the very foundations of world commerce and world prosperity. Seems to me there is something of riot in his determined knocking. How things are crumbling because we have failed to let him in! Men who yesterday were millionaires are reduced at this moment to the edge of want for the very necessities of life. Great fortunes have come tumbling to the ground. Men who yesterday reckoned their economic security as beyond all danger now feel the pressure of an unseen revolution, quiet, relentless, irresistible, that is shaking our social structure to its very foundations. We don't even know the forces that are at work. The keenest minds among the financiers, economists, and captains of trade stagger, perplexed as if blindfolded, before these illimitable forces and stand shaking as if at the middle of a storm. How we shall come out, nobody knows. The solution of our problems nobody seems able to put forward. I think he is knocking. I believe he is tired of our old selfishness and greed, of our grasping for power over one another and precedence one before another, envy and jealousy of one another. I think he is trying to get into the doors of our hearts to teach us several things.

Apparently he wants us to learn what he told us so long ago, that a man's life consists not in things and the amount of them, in bigger and bigger barns, in larger and larger bank accounts; that the beautiful life is the simple life, keen to the joys that are closest at hand, the joys of home, little or big, the joys of friendship which no greedy man can have, the joys of the beautiful world and the joys of doing things with our own hands and with our own minds in that beautiful world.

Then perhaps he wants to teach us to work harder and at smaller tasks. Men are not dying to-day from overwork; they are not shooting themselves because they have to work too long. They are dying and killing themselves because circumstances have forced them out of palatial offices and have taken out of their hands the playthings, stocks and bonds, powerful pens, command of thousands of their fellow men, and have reduced them to the ranks where, if they only knew it, they would have been far happier all this time. Economic force is to-day leveling up the herd of men and women by throwing down the mighty from their seats. They suffer under it. Change is unwelcome, but nobody knows how healthful and how salutary that change may prove to be.

He is teaching us the need of courage and good cheer. He is showing us how to pull the belt tight, to grit the teeth, to go out without money and without scrip as he sent his followers out to work and to live the simple life. He is forcing us willy-nilly, whether or no, to emulate the birds of the air and the flowers of the field. Things that we have looked upon for so long as a dreamy idealism have been brought home to our very doors. So long we have refused voluntarily to accept his teaching that now he is pouring it down our throats like medicine and we have got to take it—and like it.

Once more, it appears to me that he is showing us the need to hang together or to hang separately, to live and let live, to give and take, to work together, pull together, coöperate. We've got to put into practice his rule of life, by no means his highest admonition, to do to each other as we'd be done by. That goes for individuals, for banks and corporations, for peoples and nations. Think of that! We have begun to find out that he meant what he said, that he knew what he was about, that he was an economist right, and that only on his principles can life be lived sanely at all.

Knock, knock! Clamor, clamor! Thunder, thunder! Boom, boom!

Some of our wisest are saying these days, it's either Christ or chaos. Unless we let him in, our white civilization may come tumbling down over our heads like a decayed and ruined palace. He's knocking the door down, and knocking the walls down. Dunsinane has been besieged! Birnam Wood may to-morrow come moving upon Dunsinane. The yellow races and the brown may overthrow the structure of our Caucasian rule and flood the west, building a new empire to supplant our old. Certainly something of the kind will happen unless we learn to listen for Christ and to let him in.

It is never too late. Let conscience speak, grasp opportunity, dare to aspire, and we shall find the solutions of our problems as to how to live. Evidently, he wants us to live more simply, to work at simpler and more beautiful tasks, to give ourselves with courage and cheer to the things we have to do, with less of greed and more of human kindness and neighborliness, to take literally what he taught and apply it to our individual lives, our commerce and industry, and our relations with the other peoples of the earth. We might as well listen to his voice, or else his knocking will bring on the crack of doom.

Knock, knock! Clamor, clamor! Thunder, thunder! Boom, boom, boom!

X

LIFE'S MOST BEAUTIFUL ADVENTURE

He is not here, but is risen. LUKE 24: 6.

WHEN Charles Frohman, theatrical manager, stood on the deck of the Lusitania facing certain death, he is reported by survivors to have said to someone standing near him, "Death is life's most beautiful adventure!" He was quoting, of course, but the situation in which he stood lends added force to the words. If one can reach the mental condition in which he can utter these words with profound conviction, he has caught the finest philosophy of life. It takes a deep faith, born of much pondering, to be able to speak like that, when one knows he has only a few hours to live.

Easter, and what it stands for, gives the priceless heritage of that profound faith. Easter, the greatest day of the religious calendar, the top of the Christian year, means life, everlasting and continuous life. It means the conquest of what we have universally considered the last great enemy of man. It means not that death has no longer any terrors for us, because that would be contrary to nature; but it does mean a philosophy, founded in good

114

reason, why those terrors may be reduced almost to the vanishing point. This philosophy rests, not entirely but to a great degree, upon a strange thing that happened on this anniversary, about nineteen hundred years ago.

This is what happened: A strange young man, thirty-four or thirty-five years of age, with nothing but brave goodness in his life and benignancy in his words, scourged to the fainting point, crowned with thorns until his forehead bled, staggered under a heavy cross, along the Via Dolorosa, or Way of Sorrows, in Jerusalem, through the Damascus gate, and out to Calvary. There rough Roman soldiers drove nails through his hands and feet and lifted him upon the very cross he had borne between earth and sky. There he hung in torture for three long hours while an earthquake shook the place and clouds gathered in the skies; and though usually it took three days to kill a man this way, and though he refused to partake of a stupefying drug, he died in the middle of the afternoon. The captain of these Roman soldiers, deeply impressed by his behavior and his words on the cross, breathlessly exclaimed, "We have killed a god!" The traitor who had sold him to his enemies threw himself headlong from a cliff and killed himself. His dearest friends, including his mother, mourned him as a failure and a futility. This was on Friday afternoon.

Then on Sunday morning, the first Easter Sunday, before the dawn some women, always first at the cradle and last at the grave, came to add spices to his sepulture. They debated, as they skirted the northeastern wall of the city, coming up from the shadows of the Kedron where lay Gethsemane, as to how they should get the huge stone rolled away from the tomb. When they got there, the stone had already been rolled away, and the only light, in the surrounding obscurity, came shining out of that cave-like sepulcher. They looked in and saw nothing but a radiant angelic presence, and the graveclothes folded and laid aside. Then they heard the words, "He is not here, but is risen." They say they even saw him and thought he was the gardener and addressed him, saying, "Where have ye laid him?" To which he responded with one word, the name of his mother and of the two other women he loved best, "Mary!" Then they knew him.

Such is the story of Easter, whether literal or symbolic, that has caught the imagination of the world. I don't know that it matters much whether we think of it as a literal fact or only symbolic beauty. It does matter that the events of that morning, no matter what they were, have set the world thinking and talking about life's most beautiful adventure, and about the sure hope of immortality, as nothing else in all

history has done. Before that time, leading
prophets, philosophers, sages, had spoken in
half whispers about the deathless hope, from
Isaiah, Socrates, Confucius, on down to the immediate contemporaries of the Christ. No one
had talked with assurance, or with any degree
of certitude, until he lived, and died, and rose
again, to be everlastingly alive and dominant
in the earth. He did not undertake to prove
immortality; why should we? He did not undertake to prove God; why should we? The
most important things in human thought cannot
be proved, need not be proved. We know them
because we know them. Said Boswell to John-
son, "I think, sir, the proofs of immortality are
sufficient." Said the redoubtable doctor to his
friend Boswell, "Sir, I could wish there were
more." The Wordsworthian phrase best carries the actual state of the case, "Intimations
of immortality." These we have, so powerful
as scarcely to be gainsaid. They lend strong
possibility, not to say probability, to the undying hope. What are they?

There is the inherent desire in the human
heart, ineradicable under affliction and misfortune, for continuous and unending life. Now
no other desire springs eternal in the human
breast but somewhere and somehow has greater
or less fruition. What we incurably yearn for,
that to a slight degree at least, at the long last,

we obtain. Is it companionship, love, family?
Is it beauty, æsthetic joy, love of color, harmony
of sweet sounds? Is it intellectual satisfaction,
thought, truth? Whatever it is, to every deep-
seated, innate craving of our natures some
answer comes. Shall it be that the profoundest
of all our yearnings, the desire for endless life,
shall be frustrated? It does not seem likely.
No proof I know, but only intimation.

Then, the increasing conviction on the part of
scientific men that human thought does not de-
pend on certain physical processes in the brain;
that if all our intellectual life were conditioned
and determined for us by the purely biological
functioning of the brain, there were no room for
choice, for will, we would be automatons, machines, and nothing more. Nobody acts as if
he had no choice. Theorists may speculate as
they will, behaviorists insist as they will; but in
the very insistence they reveal their conviction
that they can choose, and their desire to make
other people choose like them. It is the height
of futility to attempt to make the human race,
or any individual of it, believe that he cannot
choose to turn round, to stand up or sit down,
to go or to come as he pleases. Nobody will
ever convince any human being that he has
absolutely no free will. And having choice,
we have something that is independent of all
physiological and biological reactions. What

is that something? That is the endless life. No proof, but a tremendous probability.

There is the further scientific fact, which we all learned as children in the schools, that no matter and no force can ever be destroyed, but only change its form. We have taken a step forward now and identified matter as force, the atom as made up of electrons, vibrating, ceaselessly vibrating, with such power that the scientists are almost afraid to try to split up an atom for fear of the damage it might do to everything in its neighborhood. No force ever goes out of existence. It may alter its drive and thrust, but it remains force still. Now here is a force, vital force, life, so strong that it directs and dominates much of the other force of the world. Shall it go entirely out of existence? Or shall it, too, only change its form? Reasoning by analogy, I know; not demonstrating, but revealing the strongest possible probability.

There is a fourth intimation which for my single self carries great weight. To others it may not be so strong, but to me it is the strongest of them all, and that is the positive statement many times repeated by that same strange young man who, though he died nearly two millenniums ago, still rules this little world as no other one personality has ever swayed it. Jesus said, "Let not your heart be troubled: ye

believe in God, believe also in me. In my
Father's house are many mansions.'' He does
not prove, he simply assumes both the Father-
God and the endless life. Then he adds, in that
simple, matter-of-fact fashion of his, as man to
man, and heart to heart, ''If it were not so, I
would have told you.'' Further he declares,
''Because I live, ye shall live also. I am the
resurrection and the life. This day shalt thou
be with me in paradise.'' Despite the strength
of these other intimations, which have for my
mind convincing value, I believe most in immortality because Jesus so quietly declared that it
was even so.

Nor, I maintain, is this the surrender of my
mind, my reason, to the dominance of an outside authority. On the contrary, we reason that
he whose words have been tested by two thousand years of human experience, as nobody
else's words have ever been tried, and have
proved so true to all that is finest and best in
human relationships, could not have been mistaken, nor deluded upon this, the most vital
question that, in life's adventure, men can ask
themselves.

These are the grounds of our hope and our
profound faith that it is not all of life to live
nor all of death to die; that we shall meet
again face to face, and know again better than
ever we knew them here, those whom we have

loved and lost awhile. We shall communicate; we shall work side by side; we shall grow and we shall play; we shall feed full every aspiration we now have after the true, the beautiful, and the good, in a career that shall go on and on and have no end. All the imagery of the final chapters of Revelation—the river clear as crystal, the trees on either side of it, the city of gold and the iridescent gates of mother of pearl—all this is feeble, grand as it is, to convey the possibilities of an unending, painless, and perfect life.

The results of this hope? Ah, they are so many and so fine. Chiefest of all, perhaps, this hope and faith gives courage to front whatever human life contains, destroys fear, lifts us up on wings above all the dismalness of our checkered fortunes in this world. In the light of this hope, we can bear so much pain and hardship, so much weariness and sleeplessness, so many hours upon the rack; for as one of the greatest sufferers of this world exclaimed, "Our light affliction, which is but for a moment, worketh for us a far more exceeding and eternal weight of glory." What William Ernest Henley bore with a stoic fortitude, we can bear, more bravely, I believe, with Christian resolution.

Privation, too, we can overtop with a faith like this. Hard times—to be sure we don't know what they are, most of us; but we can

negotiate any situation, drawing the belt tighter, clenching the teeth firmer, visualizing the
very worst that can befall us and, overriding it
before it comes, in imagination and determination, through the conviction that privation carried to its highest degree can mean nothing
more than life's most beautiful adventure. We
shall know that hard times come and go, change
and pass; and that nothing but life, force, unvarying and unending, awaits us, no matter
what the complexion of this present day.

Then we bear the separation and the losses
of those who are most precious to us in this
world, just as we bear with cheerfulness a tem-
porary separation from those who go away
upon a pleasant journey. Let this hope and
faith lay deep hold upon us, and we cannot
grieve beyond all endurance when the green
door of earth swings shut over any beloved
form. We know perfectly well that here lies
only the outworn tent, the biological brain and
body, while the real vital force has been loos-
ened and set free.

Once more, the dread enemy himself turns
into friend. When death hangs his sickle on our
garden gate, we shall be able to say, "Welcome,
friend, come in. I'll join you presently." We
shall await him resolutely, prepared and ready
for life's most beautiful adventure. Many have
waited like that. We have seen them, you and

I. We have heard them talk about it, smiling and unmoved, just as they have talked and smiled before other and lesser anæsthetics. Cherish this hope, and we shall be able to put into practice the words of Bryant, quoted in the Masonic ritual, "So live that when thy summons comes . . ." and that still finer song of the Christian's poet laureate, "Sunset and evening star . . ."

Such is the glad message of Easter. This meaning comes to us across the centuries from that first Easter morning when something strange and beautiful happened beside that rock-hewn tomb under a shoulder of Mount Calvary. The passage of the years and the rolling of the centuries only add to the impression made upon the human heart by the enigmatical events in that dim dawn. Multiplied intimations—perhaps that is almost as strong as what in the feebleness of our minds we sometimes call proof. The deep desire not likely to be frustrated, our conscious possession of choice which points the way to independence of mere bodily function, the persistence of vital force along with all other forms of force, capped by the calm utterances of the Christ—here is a weight of reasons for the hope and the faith that is within us. That hope and faith may waver at times—it does for all of us—but it comes surging back in moments of emergency

XI

UNFOUND PEARLS

EDITH WHARTON, in her story called "False Dawn," tells of a young man, Lewis Raycie, in the forties of the last century, who had just been graduated from college and sent abroad by his father. Besides ten thousand dollars for travel, the wealthy New Yorker gave his son an additional five thousand dollars with which to buy the beginning of a gallery of old masters. The father, very opinionated and domineering, knew exactly what he wanted, both for the future of his son and for his gallery. He wanted a Raphael, if possible. If not, then a Domenichino, or a Carlo Dolci, or one of Salvator Rosa's noble landscapes. The son loved a neighbor girl on the north shore of Long Island, very plain, even insignificant. Her name was Beatrice, Treeshy for short. Lewis knew his father never would consent to such a marriage for the son for whom he had such high ambitions.

Lewis went to Europe. While gazing one day upon Mont Blanc in Switzerland, he was joined by an enthusiastic and fascinating young Englishman. The latter spent his days painting the

wonderful mountains. The two young men met
at the tavern in the evening, made a convivial
night of it, and swore eternal friendship. The
young Englishman was John Ruskin. Under
Ruskin's guidance and tutelage, the eyes of
Lewis were opened to the beauty of a school of
painters older than Raphael, like Fra Angelica
and Botticelli, what has come to be known now
as the Pre-Raphaelite school of painters.
Lewis, swept by enthusiasm, spent his five
thousand dollars for some fifty pictures of this
older company of the old masters. When he
brought them home, his father was infuriated.
They represented to him nothing but daubs.
Every one of the Madonnas and the holy women
looked like that ugly neighbor girl, Treeshy
Kent. So disappointed was Mr. Raycie that he
took to his bed with a violent fit of gout and
died within the year. He bequeathed to his son
not a dollar of his estate, but only the batch of
ugly canvases.

Lewis married Treeshy. There was one
daughter. The couple spent their lives in
penury. Lewis put the pictures on exhibition
and gathered in all New York to look at them.
New York laughed and hooted. Lewis and
Treeshy died disappointed. The pictures lay
gathering dust in the garret of an ancient
maiden descendant at the end of the century.
Finally they fell into the hands of a distant heir,

a bustling young matron, who dragged one or two of them out and began washing them with soap and water. Suddenly a connoisseur from Europe, a friend of hers, happened in; seeing what she was doing, he cried out, "For God's sake, not hot water!" She had already taken half the varnish off a glorious picture. The upshot of the story is that the fifty canvases sold for five million dollars. Most of them found their way back across the Atlantic, two or three only remaining in America. The bustling young woman turned them all into limousines, furs, and a fine home. So does genius have to wait for recognition; so are our eyes holden that we cannot see the beauty that lies nearest at hand.

When I read this story I thought of another one, far shorter and far more brilliant, told by a Syrian some two thousand years ago, and recorded in a couple of verses of the thirteenth chapter of Matthew—the story of a certain merchant, seeking goodly pearls, who found one of greatest value and sold all he had to buy that jewel.

What various applications has that little story! How it is duplicated over and over, not only in the life of a broken-hearted Lewis Raycie, but in the life of every one of us to-day. Unfound pearls lie all about us. We do not need to go to Europe to find them, nor to the ends of the earth. They are in every home, every heart, just waiting to be discovered, to be understood and valued at their true worth.

The pearl is the most beautiful of all gems, the softest and the tenderest. The diamond sparkles and throws back the colors of the rainbow like a fragment of ice, but it is cold. The pearl takes the same colors, but combines and softens them; shades them gently one into another, with a combination that no diamond ever approached. A necklace of diamonds flashes you out of countenance; but a string of pearls rests and gladdens your eye. No wonder a rope of perfect pearls is worth millions. No wonder our Master chooses the pearl as the symbol of the beauties of the inner life of the kingdom of God—all the graces and purities, the gentleness and the tenderness, the strength and courage and love, the abiding glow within which knows no dimming, which mark the presence of God in a human heart.

Such pearls lie all about us undiscovered. The very soil over which we walk, no doubt, is full of them, many fathoms deep, beneath the dust and silt of centuries. One day I walked over a farm in the Ozarks, from which the young farmer had gathered up literally gallons of beautiful flint arrowheads and spearheads. And I thought, as I strolled over that place, of the dramas played out ages ago upon those hillsides and that pleasant valley. Under the fringed deerskin surged the same loves and hates, the same fears and longings, the same dumb and inexpressible desires that surge in our bosoms in this twentieth century. There lie buried innumerable aspirations after Manitou, the mighty, the God and Father of all peoples everywhere. Deep beneath the piercing of the plowshare lie the pearls of greatest price.

You may ride the roads of old settled sections of our country, and you may see the rambling log houses or the colonnaded colonial mansions, and, giving your imagination rein, you may hear the singing of the fiddles in the minuet. You may watch the powdered heads circling by the windows, or see the hooped skirts weaving in and out upon the verandas; and all their human yearnings and contentions, passions and jealousies, once more stream like the dramas before your eyes.

Nor need you go so far afield. On the streets of modern cities you may stroll along at night, looking in through the windows at the heads gathered round the family dining table or under the shaded library light, or moving in and out of hallways and doors, and you may know that in every one of those houses there are merchants seeking goodly pearls, some finding them, some only partly finding them, and some missing altogether the innermost hidden secrets of life. Or stand on the busiest corner and watch the crowds flow by, many faces tense and drawn with anxiety, many white and haggard with pain, many radiant with hope and anticipation, many placid with peace and the possession of the surest and most steadfast secret of human existence. They are all merchants seeking, trading, negotiating, yearning, hoping, fearing, despairing, concerning the pearl, the priceless pearl, the most to be valued and the most beautiful thing in all this world.

That found or unfound pearl exists somewhere for every one of us. It may be hidden in some person whom we think we know, but whom we do not and cannot appreciate. It may exist in some circumstance which seems to us hard, cruel, and inexorable. It may be in some stranger whom we see on the street or in the car every day or now and then. It may be in some task, some daily duty, that grows so tiresome year in and year out. It may be in some pain, some cross we have to bear, or some great cause for which we have to suffer, to bleed inwardly or outwardly, and finally to die. So often it knocks about the home unrecognized; so often it lies on the office desk unseen and unknown. Look for the pearl; sell all that you have and make it the supreme treasure of your life; for in it may lie the secret of the voice of God, the reign of God, in the heart and soul of a man.

One of the crown jewels of England, the greatest at its time on earth, an amethyst, lay for years and even decades a curious, rough, and irregular rock on the desk of a certain nobleman who had been a civil servant in India, where he had picked it up from the roadside in the sand. He had used it for nearly a half century as a paper weight, and many had lifted and fingered it, until at last came the seeing eye which could look beneath the surface and could see the brilliance hidden under the forbidding exterior.

Somewhere I read the dainty little story which Sir J. M. Barrie tells of his first and only meeting with Robert Louis Stevenson. Barrie, then a young student, was hurrying along toward his classes at Edinburgh University, when Stevenson bumped into him and jostled him.

Robert Louis turned round and, coming back, said, "After all, God made me."

"He is growing careless," responded Barrie.

Stevenson was tempted to give the stranger a whack with his cane; but instead he looked at him quizzically and asked, with great charm, "Do I know you?"

"No, but I wish you did," answered Barrie.

"Let's pretend that I do," said R. L. S.

Linking arms they made for the nearest tavern, talked for hours, and wound up with a furious argument over Mary Queen of Scots.

Thus did two pearls of great value to the world, by merest accident, fall into each other's company.

I knew a beautiful woman once, one of the belles of the blue grass. Her beauty well-nigh destroyed her. She married a handsome husband, who was not good for much as this world counts success. He made no great sums of money; he took no high business and social position; but he possessed something rarer than these, a gentle, sweet, and loving nature. But she saw none of these more precious attributes. She wanted success. She wanted to shine like a diamond. Imperious, querulous, embittered, she drove him out, and he came home only now and then, at long intervals, with the same sweet, quiet smile on his face. At last she learned her lesson. Far along in her middle years, her children grown and gone, she said to a dear friend of mine, ''I see it all, now, at last; but it is too late.'' She missed the pearl, the most precious thing in life, love and home and tenderness, because she simply would not see.

After all, it is in the nearest relations, with husbands and wives, with fathers and mothers, with neighbors and close associates, that the first quickening vision of the pearl is to be found. Sometimes these relations are not appreciated until it is too late; but at least they have opened our eyes to see, they have taught us in the long length of the years to understand. Love is the greatest thing in the world, in whatever form it comes—whether the love of man and woman, the love of father and son, the love of youth and comrade. It is at least the first dim discerning of the pearl of great price.

Where are we to look for this pearl, we merchants? I think I have already anticipated the answer. We are to look for it right under our feet, close at home, in the daily circle and the commonest relationships.

> "Daily with souls that cringe and flock
> We Sinais climb and know it not."

The first sight of a pearl may come to the young lad who stands by the bank of a mighty river and with awe and nameless thrill watches it go arrowing by; or as he walks in the sunlaced aisles of the forest and looks up with solemnity into their overarching boughs, the wanderlust comes aching into his soul, the call of the wild comes like a great starving into his blood. Something divine in him, a craving and a yearning answers to the deep that calls to him—deep calling unto deep. It is the glimmer of the pearl.

Poets have felt this nameless yearning. Sidney Lanier, in gravest illness, felt it as he looked out over the melancholy and, some would say, uninteresting dead level of the marshes of Glynn, for he sings:

"Tolerant plains, that suffer the sea and the rains and the sun,
   Ye spread and span like the catholic man who hath mightily
      won
   God out of knowledge and good out of infinite pain,
   And sight out of blindness and purity out of a strain."

Then higher and higher mounts the song of this man of God as a yet clearer vision comes to him of the inestimable value of God's fingers painting before him the picture of the pearl. And once again he sings:

"As the marsh-hen secretly builds on the watery sod,
   Behold I will build me a nest on the greatness of God: ...
   By so many roots as the marsh-grass sends in the sod
   I will heartily lay me a-hold on the greatness of God."[1]

This is the glow of the pearl.

Or the young father may find it, as for the first time he lays his newborn babe on his knee. The wonder of it all, the peace after the strain and the agony, the awe and the sense of a "charge to keep," may and does stir depths in him that have never hitherto been sounded. This is the shimmer of the pearl.

Or the beautiful gem may lie in the heart of that man whom you despise. He makes you tired when he comes around. You wish you'd never meet him any more. But under the forbidding exterior, deep down in the bottom-most reaches of his heart there lies a loyalty that is

[1] By permission of Charles Scribner's Sons, owners of the copyright.

like the loyalty of the dog. This is the gleaming of the pearl. "After it, after it, follow the gleam." Follow it into the heart of the man you do not like. Follow it into the friendship of the despised and rejected of men. Follow it into the hidden caverns of your neighbor's soul. There you may find the love, the comradeship, the reign of God in the soul of a man, the most precious possession in all this world.

Then you may find it in the task, maybe the daily task, maybe some worthy cause. Ah, how I have seen men transformed by some mission, some errand, some seemingly little trust and enterprise committed to their guardianship. It may have been an attempt at rescue of an erring friend. It may have been but the keeping of a door in the house of God. It may have been but the bearing of a loaf to the starving, a cup of water to the thirsty, or the paying of a visit to one sick or in prison. Yet how their faces glow with it! This is the glitter of the pearl.

Again, it may be, it is to be found in suffering, in a thorn in the flesh, in a cross, in pain. Everybody knows how pearls are made. The grain of irritating sand finds its way into the shell of the mollusk. The poor tortured creature walls it off with his own tissues and, suffering through the years, deposits upon this stranger in the flesh the precious substance which finally gleams and glows with all the iridescent beauty of a life of pain. In Japan now they cultivate pearls by deliberately introducing grains of sand beneath the covering shell of these dumb creatures of the deep. Certain it is that pain has its ministries. Recently one said to me, concerning a certain hard man of business, "What has come over that man? He is different. He is softened." I knew, but could not answer. It was the ministry of pain. This is the radiance of the pearl.

And, finally, we may find it in him who first told us about it, whose steps follow every lonely heart among mankind, whose infinite compassion never failed for those who suffer and are sad, whose love and mercy never desert those who stumble and fall, those who sin and go astray. It is ours to seek for him. Said Phillips Brooks, "Seek for your master; never be content until you find him, who by his wisdom, power, and love has the right to rule over you; then give yourself to him completely."

Having found the pearl, what is there for us to do but to sell all we have and buy it, make it ours? Nothing in life compares with it. All the comforts, the riches, the luxuries, and the preferments, are as nothing to the pearl. The presence of God, the reign of heaven within, the love that never fails, the peace that the world cannot give and cannot take away—what else is there to compare with it? It is the gleam and glow and glitter, it is the shimmer and the radiance, of the pearl. Part with everything else

XII

HIGH-POWER SALESMANSHIP

WHAT business has a preacher talking about salesmanship? Well, a preacher is a salesman. So is a lawyer. So is a doctor. So is everybody who has to use the art of persuasion. The best definition of salesmanship is the ability to persuade. To make it shorter still, salesmanship is persuasion.

I began my career as a salesman at ten years of age, when I sold, at the county fair, "score cards, programs for the races, naming each and every horse and his driver, and the color of the jockey's cap, ten cents apiece. Score cards, programs for the races." I sold so many programs that a big, burly fellow, seventeen or eighteen, threw me off the grand stand. He was selling, too, and told me not to come back. I went round to the other end of the grand stand, climbed up again, got into the middle of the crowd where he couldn't get to me, and kept on selling. I made $4 that day, and have been selling something ever since; so I claim the right to talk from experience on salesmanship.

The best classic example of salesmanship I know of is Mark Antony's oration over the dead body of Cæsar. Cæsar's friend, faced by a hostile audience, undertook to sell to them the memory of the great Julius. The men who had stabbed Cæsar—Brutus, Cassius, and the rest —made the mistake of their lives when they allowed this high-powered salesman to get access to their clients. Mark Antony does not begin attacking the quality of good which his competitors have put before the Roman people. On the contrary, he declares that Brutus and the rest are honorable men, all honorable men. Only little by little does he change his word "honorable" into a sneer and attack. At the beginning, he confines himself to the quality of goods he has to sell, the virtues of Cæsar. All the time he watches very carefully the reactions of his prospective customers. He takes them on the ground where they stand, with their prejudices, their limitations of views, and their emotional condition. His appeal contains some logic and reasoning; but for the most part it is an appeal to emotion and imagination.

A Scriptural instance of expert salesmanship is the address of Paul on Mars' Hill in Athens. He meets with a company who are eager to buy any new thing that comes along. They have never heard of his product at all; like many other buyers, they don't know what they want. They are dignified, reserved, and polished men. So St. Paul does not slop over, does not put his arm around their necks nor massage their elbows like an oily and inexpert politician. On the contrary, with a dignified restraint, he pays them a compliment, delicate and reserved, saying, "Ye men of Athens, I perceive that you are very religious people." A little further along he quotes from one of their own poets, and only gradually leads up to the good qualities of the new religion he has come to offer them. Some say that St. Paul failed at Athens, but we know that Dionysius and Damaris and several others bought his wares. If he did not obtain at once as many clients as he hoped for, he did what every wise salesman ought to do to get into other territory—he made his footwork equal to his tongue work.

Jesus recognizes the analogy between salesmanship and religious life in the parable of the talents. He says that a certain man, who was going away on a journey, turned over to his stewards a certain portion of his capital to handle for him. To one he gave ten talents, to another five, to another two, and to another one. All of them except the one who got one talent put their money out into trade, bought and sold and doubled their capital stock by the time the owner returned. Only one of them, the one-talent man, refused salesmanship. He buried his talent, which was equal to about $1,200, and refused to trade with it. All the others are commended.

Once again, Jesus recognized the arts that pertain to salesmanship when he called to certain fishermen and said, "Come, follow me, and I will make you fishers of men." He recognized the importance and the necessity of catching men, luring men, netting and hooking men. St. Paul goes to the psychological root of the same analogy when he says, "I become all things to all men, that by all means I may save some." Have you ever waded up a mountain stream or drifted down one in a boat, and whipped its waters with first one fly and then another, trying lure after lure in your attempt to make a trout or the bass rise to the hook? If you have not, you have missed one of the rarest pleasures in this world. First, you put on a gray hackle. If after a few casts you get no strike, you then change to a royal coachman. If this doesn't work, then one after another you try all the flies in your book. Or if you are after bass, on an Ozark stream, you try your red fly and pork bait; if there is nothing doing, you put on a black one, or a turkey feather; or if you are not a faithful Izaak Walton Leaguer, you will use a dowagiac minnow, a basserina, or a Tom Thumb. You are pitting your wits against those of the fish. It is a game fascinating beyond all description.

I am well aware of the limitations of this illustration. There is no analogy that is perfect. In fishing there is an element of deceit; while in the highest brand of salesmanship only truth and candor should be employed, or can prevail. You can press any illustration too far. The dressing of shop windows is like the baiting of hooks. The skillful display of goods in show cases and on shelves, what is it but the selection and combination of lures, to create wants, or to crystallize them and to catch buyers?

Now, the qualities which go to make up a good salesman are the selfsame qualities which combine to make a good citizen, a good Christian, a good man or woman. It is character that counts in all these realms; character is the whole story. You may read all the books on salesmanship—and there are a great many of them and very good ones, which it would pay any young sales person to read and study and ponder—and you may sum them all up in the one word, character. Suppose we analyze a little, however, before we begin to sum up.

Invariably all expert advice warns the sales person to be courteous. Courtesy is the very foundation of good salesmanship. To lend every consideration to your prospective buyer, to offer him a chair literally or figuratively, to make him comfortable and at ease, physically and mentally, to meet him in his own mood, and to try to bring him gradually into an amiable frame of mind if he is cross or melancholy, never to insult his intelligence, or to thrust your own peculiarities upon him offensively—this is the very foundation principle of salesmanship.

One big manufacturer who needed to change a whole system of machinery was interviewed by salesman after salesman who began with him in some such words as these: "Why, Mr. Blank, do you mean to tell me that you are still using that old worn-out system? I can't understand a man of your ability and success still holding on to that antediluvian contraption." This made the manufacturer want to argue, and he never could do business with anyone. Finally a young man came to see him who inquired courteously about his needs. When the salesman received the reply that Mr. Blank was negotiating with a certain firm of competitors and would probably close with them, he gathered up his portfolio and said: "In that event, sir, I will not waste your time, but will see several other houses while I am here. My competitor's system is a very good system, and I have no doubt you will be pleased with it." "Hold on," said Mr. Blank, "I have not closed with so-and-so. Can you come back in two weeks, and I'll see you again?" "Certainly," replied the young man; and he was back in two weeks sharp.

Meantime Mr. Blank ascertained that the young man had visited a half dozen other places in the town and had sold a couple of them.

Such courtesy is in demand. The time has gone by when any sales person, even in a big department store, can treat a customer with discourtesy and get by with it. I recollect vividly when the sales girls, in the biggest shops, used to chew gum and treat everybody with a superior and indifferent air. They even used to carry on conversation with each other while trying to sell goods—not trying either, but just lazying and soldiering on the job. Who of us does not remember conversations like this between a pair of them: "Yes, I had a date with Jimmy last night, but he didn't show up at the junction, and I seen Sammy comin' along, so I went to the skating rink with him—hully-Gee, that boy kin skate! Yes'm, that's seventy-five a yard, this is fifty. I won't waste no time on that Jimmie; any skirt can have him that wants him—all right, mam, if you don't want it, it's all the same to me—cross-grained old cat— Jimmie says he'll come to-night, but I don't care." Those dear, dead days are gone beyond recall. No such girl could hold a job in a modern, up-to-date store ten minutes.

Interest in the business of selling is another important quality for the men that meet the public to-day. Alertness and adaptability go along with interest in the art in which one is engaged. The salesman who looks upon every transaction as an artistic piece of work, who enters upon it with eagerness and zest and closes it up with satisfaction to himself and to his customer, is on the road to efficiency and happiness. He begins studying his customer before the customer has uttered one word. The modern, well-trained, high-powered salesman is not misled by any of the stock rules for judging an individual at first glance. Anybody who tells you that he can read human nature right off the bat in the first glimpse is an ass, that's all. It can't be done. There are no marks of physiognomy which are a sure and unfailing index to what is inside. Don't believe that curly hair always means so-and-so; that high cheek bones indicate this or that; that big ears or little ones, or whether the ears lie flat against the head or stand out like sails, tells anything concerning the mind or character underneath. Some old-time sales people allow themselves to make generalizations like this: "When I see anybody come in with a frown like that, I know he is not going to buy," or, "When I see a woman who uses too much rouge and lipstick, I know that she's common, and will not buy high-class goods," or, "When I see a woman in a tailored suit, I show her hammered silver." These rules are all too easy, and very fre-

proposition, or our religion. He may be cross because he has a headache, or because he is suffering indigestion, or because there is trouble back home that you know nothing about. Maybe nobody has been kind to him for a week. It is a good plan to surprise him, and a way can always be found to do it.

Persistence, footwork, trying over and over again in different ways and in different places: this, too, is a characteristic of the best salesmanship. This does not mean the forcing of a customer to take something he does not want. We are all perfectly well acquainted with that type of salesmanship which would thrust down the throat of the buyer something for which he does not care. It does mean, however, the determination to attempt the things which some regard as impossible.

> "Somebody said that it couldn't be done,
>   But he, with a chuckle, replied
> That 'Maybe it couldn't,' but he would be one
>   Who wouldn't say so till he'd tried.
> So he buckled right in, with the trace of a grin,
>   And if he worried he hid it.
> He started to sing as he tackled the thing
>   That couldn't be done, and he did it.
>
> Somebody scoffed, 'Oh, you'll never do that;
>   At least no one ever has done it.'
> But he took off his coat and he took off his hat,
>   And the first thing we knew he'd begun it.

With a lift of his chin, and a bit of a grin,
     Without any doubting or quiddit;
He started to sing as he tackled the thing
     That couldn't be done, and he did it.

There are thousands to tell you it cannot be done;
     There are thousands to prophesy failure;
There are thousands to point out to you, one by one,
     The dangers that wait to assail you.
But just buckle in, with a bit of a grin,
     Then take off your coat and go to it;
Just start in to sing as you tackle the thing
     That 'can't be done'—and you'll do it.'' [1]

>   —*Edgar Guest.*

In short, the Golden Rule is the best rule to apply. This does not mean to treat everybody as *you* yourself would like to be treated; but to treat each person as *he* would like to be treated, being who he is. Maybe you are very business-like and decisive, and you would like to be treated in a short, crisp, businesslike fashion. But your customer may be a totally different type, undecided, talkative, slow to make up his mind; then you must treat him leisurely and indulgently; give him rope and give him time. The Golden Rule intelligently applied is the best rule in business as well as in morals and religion. With the Golden Rule, of course, go absolute honesty and truth. All expert business men have begun to believe that honesty is really

[1] From Edgar Guest's book, *The Path to Home.* Copyright, 1919, by the Reilly and Lee Co. Reprinted by permission.

the best policy and that only absolute truth wins in the long run. The customer must not only go away satisfied, but he must remain satisfied. The most common fault of sales people, and the hardest to eradicate, is not that they willfully misrepresent, but that they lazily take the easiest road and gloss over the facts. This policy may attain the immediate end of making a single sale, but it does not make for the reputation of the house or the commodity.

Over and over again you hear it said that the root of the whole matter is personality. Well, what is personality? I have read many pages of glowing words by various authors about that mysterious, subtle something which we call personality. They call it that obscure and hidden force, that life-urge, and I got nothing out of the reading except a hazy, mystic groping after an unreality. Personality is simply that which makes you different from anybody else, which makes you *you*. To develop personality, then, is only to let go and be yourself. This is an easy thing to say, but an extremely difficult thing to do. So few of us know how to let go. Actors upon the stage seem to have a harder time being themselves than the rest of us. Most actors strut and swagger with a very artificial air, entirely conscious that they are in the public eye. It is only the finished actor who seems to realize that the highest skill is in being distinctly himself. Edwin Booth moved and appeared upon the stage just what he was off of it. Julia Marlowe was the same woman before an audience that she was in daily life, hence her inimitable charm. Most people are delightful underneath. If only we could penetrate beneath the mask which everybody wears and behind which everybody lives, we should find that the world is full of charming people. Now and then we say, "How charming she is!" or, "How much personality he has!" This simply means that the person in question knows how to let go, and to be out and out himself.

The world is a huge department store and life a shopping expedition. Some of us know exactly what we want; some of us feel gropingly a sense of need and know only hazily what we desire; some of us do not know at all. We can have anything in the store if we are willing to pay the price, or if we have the price to pay. Do you want above all things to be rich? All right, pay the price and you can be. It may cost you health, happiness, liberty, your soul itself; but you can be. Do you want luxury, sensuous gratification, material ends only? You can have what you want, if you pay the price and if you have it to pay. This, too, may cost health, peace of mind, your immortal soul; but pay the price and you can have it.

XIII

THE LITTLE BROWN CHURCH IN THE WILDWOOD

"Come to the church in the wildwood,
Oh, come to the church in the dale;
No spot is so dear to my childhood
As the little brown church in the vale."
(Congregation sings this text, without accompaniment.)

Most American people of middle and advancing years grew up in the shadow and under the influence of such a little church, white, red, or brown, at some crossroads not far from the wildwood. Oftentimes the little building served as school and church both, and formed the community center. All the life of the countryside, social, recreational, and religious, revolved round it. In spite of the store or post office, which was a clearing house for business and social contacts during the week, the little church held chief place because it was the only, or at least the principal, gathering place for evening and week-end functions.

The popularity of this old folk song, which has held a place for at least three generations, attests the pleasant memories which for most of us gather round the little old church. There we spoke our first "pieces," saw our first

Christmas trees, took part in our first dramatic productions, met our first sweethearts, and knew our first romance. The hitching rack for our horses, the stile block, the well, the stretch of lawn or yard, and the row of rough flagstones that formed the walk up to the door—all these bear associations for us, tender and poignant, that can never be forgot. The faces of those who influenced our most impressionable years, come crowding up before us whenever that old song is sung.

"Come to the church in the wildwood," etc.
(*Congregation singing*)

Those little churches for the most part have passed into history and tradition. The change in American conditions and customs has gradually obliterated them until very few remain. Roads and automobiles have made inevitable the consolidation of country schools and the destruction of country churches. People think nothing now of driving ten, twenty, thirty miles into the country town for social and religious contacts which at least seem more satisfying than any that can be kept up at the crossroads. The number of district schools has decreased tremedously and the number of community schools has increased. The same thing must happen and has happened to the churches. The little brown church has passed into the legendry of our pioneer days.

Along with the disappearance of the dear little old church has come the revision of the thoughts we used to have in that little old meetinghouse. Theology has undergone a change. The things taught at the crossroads with such insistence have passed. The hell-fire and the golden heaven that used to make us alternately shiver with fear or thrill with anticipation no longer are proclaimed from modern pulpits. Only in rural sections or in urban churches carrying a hang-over of the rural spirit are such doctrines taught. To be sure, much of the bucolic survives even in towns and cities. We cannot shake off in a single generation, nor in three of them, the traditions that grew up in a place so dear to us all as the little brown church. Nevertheless, as a whole the American people has sent its soul through the invisible and found out that "I myself am heaven and hell."

To preserve old traditions is wholesome for any people. Conservatism has its value; to hold on to that which is good in old manners and in old teachings is part of the whole duty of man; but to attempt to cling to ideas and usages that have gone with the passing of generations, that is the height of futility. The preaching of eternal future punishment and rewards is a vain clinging to a day that is dead. Only with intelligence therefore can we sing,

"Come to the church in the wildwood," etc.
(Congregation singing)

Because the little old church is gone, some of us jump to the conclusion that the church as a whole has about passed out. Because the population seems engrossed with motor cars, motion pictures, dance halls, and radio, it is the easiest thing in the world superficially to conclude that there is no room in the complicated social life of to-day for the church at all. Because congregations grow small, revivals disappear, preachers no longer lead and control the thought life of our communities, we can easily reach the pat judgment that the day of the church has gone with the spring wagon and the old surrey. Let us not make up our minds on too slender evidence. Let us hear something on the other side.

After all, the Church exists only to enshrine and to propagate certain ideals, the teachings of Jesus. How do those ideals fare to-day? That is the evidence we ought to gather in this case. Do they grow or do they diminish? I admit that only reluctantly does society entertain those ideals, but I insist that, however reluctantly, society increasingly finds itself thrown back upon those ideals as the only means of safety and well-being. Our big business men and our economists to-day find themselves totally unable to grapple with the complicated conditions of modern life, suddenly become urban

instead of rural, just because they try so hard
to repudiate those ideals of Jesus as applied to
modern business, industry, and international
relations.

Faintly and feebly some business men and
some economists begin to grasp the fact that no
future exists for us, no prosperity and no
safety, unless and until we begin applying the
social program of Jesus to the bewildering conditions of our modern times. The Golden Rule
must come into play before we shall ever get
rid of our depressions. Industry must be content to give a just share of its profits to the
hand workers who produce those profits.
Every man who wants to work must have an
honest chance to work. The men at the top as
well as at the bottom must learn that a man's
life consists not in the abundance of the things
that he possesses—money, power, control of
the lives of others.

All of us must learn from the birds and the
flowers that used to cluster round the little
brown church in the wildwood that it is the
height of extravagance and foolishness to be
anxious for the morrow, what we shall eat and
drink and wherewith we shall be clothed.
These simple and elemental teachings of the
Nazarene, the essential things taught in the
little crossroads church, I tell you these are the
most needed messages in the great metropolis,

in the stock exchanges, in the halls of government the world over. There can be no peace, let alone prosperity, until we begin to put them into practice. In that sense we can sing with all the power in us and all the enthusiasm,

"Come to the church in the wildwood," etc.
(*Congregation singing*)

Now then, do you suppose that the institution, and the only institution, that holds these secrets can lose its place? Do you agree with the snap judgments of the little reporters and magazine writers who declare that the day of the Church is done? Then indeed you are doing some rather superficial thinking. Over and over in history the same snap judgment has been passed upon the Church; and over and over the clouds that obscured it have rolled away and there it has stood revealed, fairer, stronger, more influential than ever. To what a degradation did the Church sink in the Middle Ages, with all the corruption of its clergy, the luxury and the selfishness and the debauchery from the highest to the lowest. No wonder men thought that it tottered to its fall. But through the fires of revolution and reformation, the Church and all its branches came out refined, more powerful than ever.

Do not judge by numbers alone the influence of the Church in the present day. Not majorities but minorities have ever done the thinking and the leading for the masses of purblind men and women. Grant that the churches are not crowded, grant that the clergy no longer hold absolute sway over the minds and hearts of crossroads communities or great city slums and boulevards, grant that the Church does not control business, the press, the favorite amusements of millions. None the less the quieter voice of the persistent few who see and understand the only secrets that can solve the problems of our modern life comes whispering, if not thundering, that secret into the slow comprehension of those who hold power in our time. Fear not, little flock, you hold the key. It is God's good pleasure to give you the kingdom.

"Come to the church in the wildwood," etc.
(*Congregation singing*)

The old religion of fear went out with the crossroads church. The present-day interpretation of Christianity finds in it not fear but love of life and everything fine in life. We no longer shrink from life, but we walk up to it and shake hands with it and embrace it. We say, "Good day to you, Life, how do you come on? What have you got for me to-day? Show me, Life, the best thing I can do and be to-day." We experiment; we try all things and hold on to

what is good. We do not fear nature, but we
love it. We go out into it and we say, "How
do you do, Nature? You are looking lovely
to-day. I like you when you are hot, because
I have ice to cool me off. I like you when you
are cold, because I have fire and woolens and
furs. You are pretty terrible at times, you
lovely creature, Nature, but I am trying to
learn how to get along with you to best ad-
vantage. In spite of bugs and insects and
germs, old Nature, you are beautiful, even when
terrible, and I am not afraid of you. I am in
love with you."

Yes, we are not afraid of God. We fear God
only in the Biblical way, in the sense of trust
and friendship. We are in love with God. We
turn our faces up or outward or inward, or in
whatever direction we think he is, and we say,
if we have caught the modern spirit, "God, how
do you do? It looks to us on first glance as if
you make a great many mistakes. You mar a
great many pots in the making. We'd say
offhand that the hand of the potter shook. But
we think of it in another way: maybe you didn't
make the mistakes, but we did. You have made
much better machines than we could ever make,
whether it is the anatomy of a butterfly or a
bird, or whether it is that queer and intricate
system of differentials and transmissions, pipes
and cylinders which we call man. You are a

considerable artist, God, and we love your work. We love you.'' Not fear of life but love, love of all things fair and true and good. That's the modern note which occasionally was struck far back yonder in the little brown church, but increasingly is struck in the city churches of our time.

Those who love the little brown church and its memories need have no fear for the changed Church of our changing civilization. We are passing from one age into another, no doubt about that, but the Church in the very nature of the case, the repository for the only solvent idea in our bankruptcy, must survive and must grow in influence. It has lived for two thousand years through all sorts of storms and tempests, through all kinds of changes of thought and manner. It will not perish under the strain and stress of our time. ''Our little systems have their day; they have their day and cease to be.'' But the Church goes on and will go on forever. Not that in itself the Church is a thing of such supreme value, but that it holds the thing of supremest value.

I am not concerned with the changes in the church, from the little brown one into the big red one in the country town or the huge cathedral in the city. I don't care about the changes in its nonessential doctrines, from the hell-fire day to the day of inward aspiration; but I am concerned, passionately concerned, with the preservation of the teachings of Jesus, those blazing jewels for which the Church is only the casket. Change the casket as often as you please, the jewels remain the same. We've got to change it. We can no longer keep on with little brown methods in a big, dashing, daring social setting. We've got to lay aside country-jake methods for metropolitan ways and manners; but all these things cut little ice compared with the diamond facets of those gems of Jesus we have to keep and show. The institution of the Church is necessary in an institutional world, but it is secondary, unimportant as to its form and appearance, compared with the value of that which is enshrined. Let us sing, then, with discrimination, the old folk song,

"Come to the church in the wildwood," etc.
(*Congregation singing*)

Not a bad thing, then, to look back over the passage of the years, to remember tenderly those old scenes, old faces, sad and happy old days, when we all went to the country church because it was the only place we had to go to. It is a wholesome thing, however, to face the fact that the old day and the old church have forever gone, and with them many of the ideals that formed the spring of our conduct and our thought; wholesome to realize that fear in our religion has given place to open-faced aspiration for fine living and thinking; wholesome to consider that the Church, important only as the custodian of the ideas of Christ, is only moulting, changing its feathers, shedding its fur, for a new springtime and is not sick with a mortal disease; wholesome and sensible to look conditions fairly and squarely in the face, not grieving for a day that is dead, but pulling our belts up tight for a day that is just being born.

XIV

THE LIFE CREED OF ROBERT LOUIS STEVENSON

To be honest; to be kind; to earn a little and to spend a little less; to make on the whole a family happier for his presence; to renounce when that shall be necessary and not be embittered; to keep a few friends, but these without capitulation; above all, on the same grim conditions, to keep friends with himself—here is a task for all that a man has of fortitude and delicacy.[1]

ROBERT LOUIS STEVENSON.

To get in a single paragraph any man's philosophy of life, particularly a man of the stamp of Robert Louis Stevenson, is a rare privilege. Born under the damp, dour skies of Scotland; with his frail body battling all his life for breath itself, let alone health; only late in his short career finding a kindly climate in far-away Samoa; perfecting himself as a stylist as few of our English race have done; and all the time producing in spite of the agonies of body and mind his beautiful literature, we may well profit by what he considers the secret of brave and skillful living. He gives it to us in this nutshell. Let us analyze it.

"To be honest." The world has learned, to a

[1] By permission of Charles Scribner's Sons, copyright owners.

degree, that honesty in business is the best policy. A good salesman tells the exact truth about what he has to sell, and nothing but the truth. It never pays to sell under false pretenses. Even yet, however, business people keep butting their heads against the stone walls of dishonesty, spurred on by the relentless competition of our time. Business houses tread the verge of the precipices of deceit and illegality, and keep lawyers with the sole purpose of directing them along the dizzy edge. Business can never be most successful and most prosperous, nevertheless, until it learns the lesson not only of honesty but of actual coöperation. Dimly, leaders in business begin to see that, not merely with regard to competitors and with other lines of business, but also with regard even to foreign nations.

To be honest involves, moreover, the personal habit of meeting all obligations, paying all debts. No man is worthy of the respect of his fellows who does not pay his debts, clean up to the hilt. The very foundation of morality in a social world lies in the most scrupulous honesty in all dealing with money. Many people make a great effort to pay as few debts as possible and to be as slow as they can about paying them. They even do that with their church pledges. Our country, perhaps more than any other, on account of the installment system, comes as near falling into the immorality of wriggling out of the honest payment of obligations as any people can. One of the phases of our so-called hard times lies just in that, the heavy burden of advanced pledges for all kinds of luxuries under which our people struggle, and the desperate attempt to get out of paying it. No nation can be happy in that condition.

To be honest, however, goes deeper than money matters reach. To be honest implies the telling and the living of the truth. Now, nobody but tells white lies. Human society would be almost unbearable if everybody spoke out his innermost thoughts on all occasions. We all know pestiferous persons who pride themselves on telling their friends, in season and out of season, the unvarnished truth. People have to tell little social fibs, and they do not count; they simply save the face of somebody. Doctors often cannot tell the unvarnished truth to their patients; if they did they would retard recovery and even hasten death. Remember the test question posed by William James, "Would you tell the truth to a band of robbers asking you which way an intended victim went?" Of course you wouldn't. That is not the kind of honesty that R. L. S. is talking about. He means sincerity, naturalness, transparency, the being, down deep in you, of the thing you appear to be on the surface. Simplicity of bearing, straightforwardness, living out plainly what is inside—that is a job which calls for character.

"To be kind." In our swift passage through this world it takes attention and effort to deal kindly with the people we pass by. So much easier to jostle them, bump into them, knock them off their feet. We are in a hurry; there's no time for civility, let alone kindness. To live in a house by the side of the road and be a friend to man demands leisure, demands thought, demands imagination. To treat everybody alike, and to treat all kindly, ah, that is a real task. Such an easy thing to feel repulsion for somebody because he has said or done something we do not like, or because he looks like some disagreeable person we knew years ago, we can't even think who; therefore we treat him brusquely.

Easy to be kind? I say it is hard. So much easier to be unkind. We miss the law of kindness in our struggle to be just. We would deal with everybody according to his deserts—then who of us would 'scape whipping? I say it calls for imagination, the power to see into the other person's heart, thought, motive, the power to put oneself in another's place and to do as we would be done by. The trouble with us all is, we can't understand how other people act the way they do; hence we have no tolerance for the strange things they say and the strange things they do. You can see now what a big job R. L. S. marks out for us.

"To earn a little, and spend a little less." In our country our ambition is to earn a whole lot and spend a whole lot more. How many people live beyond their incomes and complain of the hard times. He does not say to inherit a little, but to earn it. No such good money as the money we make. With our own hands, with our own brains, to sell our product or our services and get a just return, however small, that is profound satisfaction. Prices, they say, are coming down, and wages are coming down. Very well, we shall be just about even when the whole thing is leveled up. We have got to learn, like the older nations, to be content with earning only a little. The president of the Chicago Great Western said the other day that this depression will never end until America learns to think internationally. There is more in that expression than appears on the surface. America possesses so much wealth and power that she can affect economic conditions all over the world. When she refuses to think in world terms, and continues to think only in terms of herself and her selfish isolation, she only promotes hard times for herself and for all the world.

Economy, too. There comes the Scotch strain

into the life philosophy of Robert Louis. Well
for us if that strain developed in every one of
us. Save a little; not much, but a little. Pay
up all honest debts, every last one of us, for we
cannot begin to be Christians until we do that;
and then lay aside a little for some future
emergency. Mr. Coolidge preached economy.
The government did not really economize much
under his administration, but the preaching was
worth while. It left an indelible imprint on the
thought of the nation.

"To make on the whole a family happier for
his presence." Before you can make a family
happier, you must belong to a family. If you
are a minor, your best chance for happiness lies
in cultivating father and mother, brothers and
sisters, and adding a little bit to their happiness. If you have reached your majority and
are cut loose from a family, then your best
chance of happiness is to scurry around and
start a family of your own. That goes for almost everybody. There are always some exceptions; but by and large your bachelors, male
and female, take a chance. A time will come
for them when they cannot fulfill this life creed
of R. L. S. There will be no family for them to
make happier by their presence.

Note the qualifying phrase, "On the whole."
Evidently here is a concession to the imperfections of human nature. He does not expect us

to be unvarying Pollyannas, little tin angels. Sometimes we just can't help making a family unhappy by our presence. Suppose we catch the flu. The family is bound to be disturbed; they may even catch it from us. Suppose we are bilious, and don't know it, we say and do things that at other times we wouldn't say and do. We make the family unhappy, just can't help it. It is not really our fault unless we have eaten too much or eaten the wrong things; then it is our fault. "On the whole"—we thank you, R. L. S., for recognizing the weaknesses of us all. Most of the time, then, we can and should brighten the place where we live, even if it is only a boarding house family. People we come into contact with, ought to be happier for the contact. Consideration, gentleness, thoughtfulness for the comfort and the welfare of those round us, no sulks, no blues, no taking it out on the folks at home because things have gone wrong at school or down town, or because the employer has been unjust, unfair, irritating. These things are as catching as the flu, but unlike the flu we can choke them off and refuse to pass them on. The family, that's the place to sing, whistle—unless there is somebody there who thinks you can't whistle and doesn't like to hear you try—the place to play, to dance, to listen to the radio, and to laugh. Oh, the family is the place for all sorts of relaxation and good

times. Don't be a spoil-sport. Take a hand in
the fun. R. L. S. used to play on the floor for
hours with little lead soldiers with the children.

"To renounce when that shall be necessary,
and not be embittered." We all renounce; we
have to; but to do so without being embittered,
that is another matter. Our renunciation usually carries so much of disappointment that we
allow the dregs of bitterness to settle in the
heart and tinge the whole color of our lives.
We make life doubly hard for ourselves and for
those about us. To give up a picnic or a party
or a picture show—what a world of bitterness
such a renunciation may create in a child's
heart. That is because the child is a child, has
not grown up. Some never do grow up. Life,
which is one series of disappointments, ham-
mers upon such a person all in vain; it brings
no education, no development. The child remains a child to the end. On the other hand,
some of the most beautiful lives you and I have
known are those which have had to give up
their hopes one by one, have accepted the inevitable, and have made the best of what was
left to them.

"To keep a few friends, without capitulation." Not to make a whole lot of friends.
Almost anybody can do that who will go around,
hail-fellow-well-met, slapping people's backs
and massaging people's elbows. R. L. S.

doesn't mean that. He means to go through this world looking for real friends; just a few of them, for nobody ever has many, no matter how "popular" he may appear to be; friends that stick closer than a brother, friends and their adoption proved, worthy to be bound to you with hoops of steel, friends who know you through and through and love you in spite of their knowledge, friends you can count on through thick and thin. Deep pathos it is to be disappointed in one whom you thought to be such a friend; and all too frequent this pathos in human life. "He was my friend, faithful and just to me." That is the highest tribute one man can pay to another.

If you have to compromise, capitulate, give up your individuality to hold a friendship, then it is no real friendship. That is what R. L. S. means by the phrase "without capitulation." If your friend is your friend, you do not have to act a part in his presence. You do not have to give up yourself and your personality. On the contrary you can be most openly yourself, and know that he will prize you all the more, because of that very abandon. To thyself be true—old Polonius agrees with R. L. S.

Just a few friends, a very few, four or five, two or three, sometimes only one—there is the circle for the really happy life. Not at the center of a swirling throng of followers, not moving about amongst a host of acquaintances; but quietly, relaxed, at ease, with a few friends, every one of whom you can trust to the extreme limit, that is the garden spot of the world. It does not make for happiness in this world to be the observed of all observers, to be recognized everywhere you go, to be pointed out, to be talked about. We all think that this does make for happiness; and we only cheat ourselves when we think so. How tickled we are when our names get into print! That happiness is only momentary, passing, deceiving. The real happiness lies in the quietude of the small circle of friends that stay to the end.

"On the same grim conditions, to keep friends with himself." Perhaps it is easier to keep friends with some of the others than always to be at peace with oneself, to respect oneself, to be in harmony with oneself. So obstinate, so obstreperous, so constantly deluded we are, that we alienate ourselves, offend ourselves, refuse to be friends with ourselves. Hard, isn't it, always to keep our heads up because we are not ashamed of ourselves? Not merely the things we do but the things we fail to do, the one-half efficiency, the cowardice that holds us back from the daring word we ought to speak and the daring thing we ought to do, that keeps us from respecting ourselves.

"On the same grim conditions." That means

no capitulation, no surrender, no compromise with ourselves and our own ideals, no refusal to think, say, act, as the inner imperative would urge us to do. No bargaining and making terms within ourselves, no backing and filling, but driving straight ahead. To strive, to seek, to find, and not to yield! Like Ulysses. No shilly-shallying in the face of that mob, whatever the mob, whatever the horde of obstacles or enemies. Yes, that calls for heroism in what we think to be an unheroic day.

That little life creed, first time you read it, sounds so gentle, so mild, so easy to fulfill. But think it over, friend, test yourself by it, and see how well you carry it out. I know of One young man who fulfilled it to the utmost of his short life, shorter than Stevenson's. He lived only to thirty-three, the center always in his last three years of swirling crowds, and done to death by bitter enemies. He kept his honesty, his kindness; he worked with his hands for thirty years to earn a little; he made his family happier, on the whole, though he caused them some unavoidable distress; he kept a few friends, ah, very, very few, to the end; and he never failed to keep his self-respect. Such a life does indeed call for all the fortitude, the courage, the heroism, as well as the delicacy of touch, the artistry of execution, that any one man may possess.

XV

START WHERE YOU STAND

I⊤ is reported that Henry Ford is accustomed to say to any man who begins work for him, "Start where you stand." By this he means that the man's past is not of interest to his new employer, that there is no use going into ancient history, that Mr. Ford is not concerned with autobiography and very little concerned with references. Whatever the past has been, this new relationship is purely *de novo;* every man must stand on his own feet, not on the shoulders of former friends, and is to be valued for himself alone, not for his connection or his heredity. Neither are his past aberrations of thoughts or conduct to count against him. Here is a new, fresh, clean start in life and work.

Now the wisdom of Mr. Ford's administration of his great business is not here in question. Whether his paternalism is in the long run to make for the ill or the good of industry is a question too complicated for most of us to decide, possibly even for Mr. Ford to decide. The passage of years alone may be able to answer that inquiry. What we are here concerned with is the wisdom of this one particular aphorism,

173

"Start where you stand." St. Paul, in Philippians 3, seems to agree with Mr. Ford when he says, "Forgetting the things which are behind," and Jesus seems to agree also when he says, "Let the dead bury their dead."

St. Paul is using the figure of the race. He insists upon a quick start and no looking back for the runner who would make the goal and win the race. St. Paul knew something about the rules of athletics. At the Olympic Games in France, one American runner, Charles Paddock, in the 400 meter dash, just at the tape suddenly turned his head ever so little and for just a moment, and lost his race. Lot's wife did the same thing with lamentable results. And when Jesus says to the man who wanted to follow him but who first desired to go home and bury his father, "Let the dead bury their dead. Follow thou me," he meant no hard, cruel, unnatural attitude toward parents, but he meant simply to show that in so vital a thing as a complete change of life and a new start, there must be no repining, no waste of time, no vacillation of will. He meant just what he meant on another occasion when he said, "Let not him that putteth his hand to the plow look back." No man can drive a straight furrow, any more than he can run a winning race, while looking over his shoulder.

"Let him that putteth his hand to the plow not look back,
 Though the plowshare cut through the flowers of life to its
     fountains,
 Though it pass o'er the graves of the dead and the hearts of
     the living,
 'Tis the will of the Lord, and his mercy endureth forever."

Nevertheless, there are some limitations to one's ability to begin at any time in his life with a clean slate, to blot out the past entirely, to start where he stands. Indeed, if one should attempt to sum up the whole matter he would be compelled in all truth and candor to make a statement somewhat like this: in a way you cannot start where you stand, and in a way you can start where you stand; anyway, you ought to try to start where you stand.

To maintain that anybody at any time without qualifications can start where he stands is to ignore the influence of heredity, the power of environment, and the irrefragable effect of past experience. To be perfectly fair and honest about it, everyone of us is limited in his ability to make a fresh start by at least these three elements in every human life. "Blood will tell" is a statement that we know to be equally true of men and animals. It takes a horse with a lineage to win races; it takes a bird dog bred to the purple to win in field trials; it takes a vegetable with a long ancestry to take the prize in exhibitions. Search the pages of Who's Who, and compare them with the census reports, and you will find that sons of distinguished men have themselves the best chance for distinction. It may surprise you to learn that the sons of ministers, proverbially the worst boys in town, have the best chance of anybody for distinction. Doubtless this is not all due to heredity, but some of it is to environment. It is not always easy to draw the line. Neither does blood always tell, for, more's the pity, there are many ignoble sons of noble fathers; but taken by and large it has been well established on scientific grounds that there is a vast deal in heredity.

When all is said and done, however, there is plenty of experience to prove that one may rise superior to unfortunate or limited inheritance. There is far too much saddling of our poor buried ancestors with the sins and derelictions of their distant progeny. Very few of us have any right to lay our own mistakes and failures at the door of our dead and buried granddads. In the last analysis we shall none of us ever get fair and just praise or blame for what our fathers were. It is an inexorable law of this hard-headed and practical world that every tub must stand on its own bottom.

More powerful than heredity in limiting our freedom is the environment in which we grew and the history of our past life. We are just beginning to understand in all its full force the importance of the first seven years of any child's life. Was there in that period a tyrannical and arbitrary parent, or a doting and over-indulgent one? If so, the results may often be disastrous and the child's nature forever be warped. Or was there at school in these early years a czar or an ogre of a teacher? Scars may have been made on the soul of the child which never in a long lifetime can be fully eradicated.

The patients who come to our psychiatric clinic are many of them instances which go to prove the statements just made. In the hospital now we have a man of middle years who was an only son, spoiled to death when he was little, and spoiled ever since, with such results that he is suffering from an actual lesion of a vital organ. It would be very difficult for him to start where he stands. The foolishness of a doting mother and perhaps of an overindulgent wife have so affected him that he can never shake off the results. The best he can do from this out is to limp along only a half a man.

I could give a number of other such instances if it were not that the people live right round here and might be too easily identified. Suppose I go over into Ohio for illustration. Dr. Waters, of Lakeside hospital, told me of a patient of his, a boy, who was swinging a scythe cutting weeds when suddenly he struck an especially tough bunch, wrenched his back, dropped his scythe, and went home to bed. The doctor, when summoned, examined him, found nothing out of place but only a muscle strained, and told him to stay in bed three or four days and he would be all right. His mother, a dour old Scots woman, wailed: "No, he will never be all right again. My brother did just the same thing and he never could get over it as long as he lived."

That boy stayed in bed eighteen months. Every now and then they summoned Dr. Waters. He always told them there was nothing the matter with the boy, that he ought to get up and dress and go to work; then the father and mother both would curse and malign the doctor and all but drive him off the place. One morning about four o'clock there came a violent knocking on the doctor's door. He hurried down in slippers and bathrobe and there stood the boy, crying breathlessly, "Come quick! Pa thinks ma is dying!"

"How did you get here?" It was a mile and a half.

"Walked," replied the boy; "the horses were all down in the back pasture. It was harder to catch one than to walk."

The old mother died and the boy got entirely well. Here is a plain case of suggestion, and of too much mother. It would be a great deal

better for a lot of children in this world if, like
Topsy, they "jest growed." We make such an
important job of "raising" children. How
could anybody raise a child anyhow? The child
raises itself and a good part of the time he
would do a lot better job of it if he were left
alone to do it for himself. Too much fooling
with a young sapling or a delicate flower sprout
easily twists it awry, dwarfs it, or kills it. So
with all the fussing and fuming and over-zeal-
ous "raising" of children. There are, after
all, not very many who have been free enough
in their formative period to be able now to start
where they stand.

And what shall be said concerning the ineradicable record of our own choices and acts
upon the tissue of our souls? Much of that
tissue is scar-tissue. Each one of us is the
product of his past history. The warp and woof
of the soul as it stands to-day is the sum of
those patterns, multitudinous and intricate,
woven into it by all the past perceptions,
thoughts, and acts. Much as we should like to
erase some of these from our being, it cannot
be done. How often, in the jails and the prisons, men and women would be glad to give a
right arm to be rid of some of that past experience. The lawyers' favorite stanza from Omar
Khayyam is this:

"The moving finger writes; and having writ,
　Moves on; nor all your piety nor wit
　　Shall lure it back to cancel half a line
　Nor all your tears wash out a word of it."

To the clinic again.　Months ago I was summoned to the home of a woman, not a member of this Church but of another.　She was lying on a couch, moaning, haggard, a wreck of what was once plainly a beautiful woman.　She had her whole family in hot water day and night and gave nobody any peace or rest.　She could scarcely walk and was capable of no household duties.　Two of us, one on each side, managed next day to get her into a motor car and bring her to the clinic to consult the psychiatrist.　An hour's conversation with the doctor revealed a liaison of several years' standing, a conscience torn to ribbons, and a pain in the mind almost impossible to bear.　The woman's face was seamed and scarred like the face of a Medusa; her eyes burned in deep, dark sockets; none the less she was beautiful.　Months rolled by.　The doctor did all he could for her and evidently did much, for the other day she came into the clinic by herself, a smile on her face, the first I had ever seen there, walking freely and easily.　She was still haggard, there were still dark rings beneath her eyes, but those big eyes shone now with a new light.　She said: "I am better; oh, so much better.　I have taken up my life again

where I left it off. I am back in my Church.
I am at work.''

Of course, she can never be just the same
woman she was before tragedy came into her
life. She can and she cannot start where she
stands; but she can reconstruct her life, reëdu-
cate her soul. She can begin over, though she
can never forget.

An old physician once said to me, "No man
can die a consistent Christian with a pain be-
low the diaphragm.'' It certainly is true that
no one can live a consistent Christian with a
pain in the mind, a conflict in the soul. Another
rough-spoken physician more recently said to
me, "No man can play hell all his life and expect to be in heaven in his old age.'' By which
he meant that no man can sow dragon's teeth
and the whirlwind all through youth and middle
age and expect serenity, peace, and calm as the
casement grows a glimmering square. I do not
believe in future everlasting punishment. I do
not believe in a lake of fire and brimstone. I
am a universalist in the long, long run; but I
do believe in hell. There are people in hell now,
thousands of them, for I have seen them.

Now to turn to the brighter side of the picture, in a way and with limitations one can start
where he stands. One can shake loose from the
past. One can begin all over again. St. Paul
and Jesus both have given very clear intima-

tion, yes, even assurance, that since we are all
at most infants, we can at any time begin re-
construction, reëducation, redemption. Jesus
cared nothing about the thefts and the usuries
of Zacchæus. He said, "This day is salvation
come to this house." Start where you stand.
He ignored the past history of the woman of
Samaria after he had shown her that he knew
it, and sent her to spread the news of the Great
Physician in the city of Sychar. He cared
nothing for the denial of Simon Peter, but said
to him, "Feed my sheep." He cared nothing
for the cowardice and defection of all the
twelve, but said to them afterwards, "Ye shall
be witnesses unto me."

Jesus came to teach the world—thank God
that he did—that a broken, truncated life may
be taken up and made into a thing of beauty
and of joy. St. Paul caught his view and declared that we all are but babes in Christ, and
it doth not yet appear what we shall be. Moreover this good news of redeeming power and
love is altogether in harmony with the findings
of the most recent science of the mind. We
used to say, "Habit is a cable. We weave a
thread of it each day, and it becomes so strong
that we cannot break it." We know better now.
Habit is a cable; but careful, patient picking at
it, strand by strand, will break it; and careful,
patient weaving will produce a new cable just as

strong and possibly in the long run stronger than the old one. There is a land of beginning again, there is a fresh page for anyone of us who wants it. Earth has a joy unknown in heaven, the new-born joy of sins forgiven. Tears of such pure and deep delight, O angels, never dimmed your sight.

We used to sing in revival meetings when I was a boy a foolish hymn which ran, ''The bird with a broken pinion never soared so high again.'' We know better than that. We know that some birds have soared higher than ever after their pinions have been broken. We don't know how high they might have soared if they had never met with accident. But certainly they went higher than they had ever gone before. What about Augustine, who, after a wild and riotous youth, turned saint? What about Tolstoi, who followed exactly the same road? Would Shakespeare ever have soared where he did without the broken pinion of an unhappy home? Where would be our John B. Goughs, our General Booths, our John G. Woolleys— birds with a broken pinion every one of them!

Dr. Henry Oldys of Maryland, the bird man, is authority for this incident. A boy threw a stone and broke the wing of a mother robin, which had a nest full of young in a farmer's yard. The cock robin seemed very young and inexperienced; it was probably his first brood;

at any rate he appeared helpless in the emergency. According to Mr. Oldys, it takes fourteen feet of earthworm per day for every baby robin. The poor mother with the broken wing was helpless to fly up to her little ones and it seemed inevitable that they should perish. The thoughful farmer, however, placed a ladder against the tree leading up to the nest; and the mother, seizing an angleworm, availed herself of the ladder, hopping from rung to rung and making her way to her babes. Undaunted by her affliction, she set industriously to work and she had to work very hard. She began before dawn in the morning and continued until 'way after dark at night. Hundreds of people drove in from all the surrounding country to see the tireless little mother bird at work; and the result was that ten thousand new members in the state of Nebraska were added to the Audubon Society, whose purpose is the protection of song birds. Here was a bird with a broken pinion which accomplished a work for her kindred that no normal bird could ever have done. Is not the same thing indicated over and over in human experience?

The important thing, after all, is that everyone of us should try. Indeed, trying is the most important thing in life. It is not so much succeeding as it is trying that constitutes life. When anybody has ceased trying he has ceased living. The psychologists are telling us these days that the essence of human life is ever and always to become. Life is a becoming. Death and sin are ceasing to become. The unpardonable crime is to stop growing, which means to stop trying. So whether we can start where we stand or whether we are held back by our past is not the question. The thing is to try, to be always starting, always trying, always becoming—that is the manifest obligation as well as the manifest joy and inspiration in human life.

One of the commanders in our Civil War—it sounds like Phil Sheridan—watched for some time a Confederate battery which was playing havoc with his lines. He called to him a captain and said: "Captain, will you take that battery?"

"I'll try, sir," replied the Captain.

Sheridan struck one gloved hand into the other and repeated: "Captain, will you take that battery?"

"I'll try, sir."

A third time and more intensely the general thundered at the young officer: "Captain, will you take that battery?"

"I'll do it or die, sir."

"Very well, Captain, go on."

Two brave Englishmen lost their lives trying to conquer the summit of Mount Everest, that unconquerable mountain which lifts its head above the Himalayas twenty-six thousand feet above the level of the sea. To the top of that mountain no human foot has ever gone. It stands there a perpetual challenge. The leader of this English expedition, Leigh Mallory, when last he was in America, was greeted with the question: "Why do you want to climb Mount Everest?"

"Just because it's there," was the laconic reply.

"Just because it's there!" Just because it is unconquerable, just because the storms swirl perpetually around its summit, just because its brow frowns and threatens, just because it is something nobody has ever done—that is sufficient reason for trying with all one's might to accomplish the hitherto impossible. It is worth laying your life down for—well worth it. It is as well worth conquering as the Poles for which so many good men have laid their lives down. The success is not the important thing. It is the trying, the striving, the fighting on. Everyone of us has before him a goal, just as difficult, just as complex, as the summit of Mount Everest or the South Pole. It is for us, then, to be up and at it, to start where we stand, to forget the things which are behind.

XVI

GO BACK WHERE YOU LOST IT

A CLASSIC story, told by Euripides—or maybe it was Herodotus—concerning a certain small city in Attica—or maybe it was Oklahoma, I forget which—explains that the city was too little to possess lights on every corner. It was only on every other corner that it boasted a lamp-post. A certain citizen of that community had been out rather late at night, engaged in the worship of Bacchus, and evidently was on his homeward way when a friend found him holding to a lamp-post and scrutinizing the ground intently within the circle of light. The friend said to him: "What's matter, Sam, lost something?"

"Yesh. Losht my watch!"

With the usual inanity that characterizes our questions in such emergencies, the friend inquires: "Where did you lose it? Right around here?"

"No. Losht it back at that other corner."

"Well, why don't you go back there and hunt for it?"

"'Cause there ain't no light back there."

There is no use looking for a thing where you

187

did not lose it. Unless it is something alive that can move away, you'd better go back where you lost it. The only place to search for lost valuables is the place in which they were originally lost. Anybody in his right mind would know this fact. The trouble with this citizen was that he was in no condition to be entirely reasonable in his conduct.

There are a great many of us, however, just as lacking in wisdom as he. We insist on searching for valuable things we have lost, not in the place where we lost them, but somewhere else. Perhaps we have lost peace of mind, or courage, or self-respect, or happiness; and we do not follow the perfectly evident and sensible course of going back where we lost them, but persist in going further and further afield, getting deeper into the mire, and refusing to turn back.

Jesus told the story of a woman who lost one of her wedding coins. The women of the Orient wear bands of collected coins, gold or silver according to their social status, round their necks or round their foreheads. To lose one of these coins is calamity, no less; for these coins mean more than just so much intrinsic value. They mean home, husband, children, destiny. A woman of our Western world could better afford to lose all her diamonds than a woman of the Orient her coins of dowry. This woman whom Jesus tells about did not rush crying calamity through the streets, nor hasten to the well where the women foregather to bewail her loss; but she lighted a lamp, looked in all the dark recesses of the house, and swept carefully the littered mud floor of the dwelling where she had lost the coin, until she found it. Then she called her friends in to rejoice with her. Jesus said this coin represented the Kingdom of Heaven or the Reign of Heaven, it represented those very things which we so easily lose and which we refuse to hunt where we lost them— peace of mind, self-respect, courage, and happiness.

Jesus told another story, about a sheep herder who when at night he led his sheep into the fold or into the open sleeping place in the pasture missed one of them. Without delay he left the ninety and nine where they were and went back to where he had lost that one. He searched every gorge and mountainside where the flock had been that day, until at last he found the poor bewildered creature, bleating in the night. Then he took it up in his arms, laid it across his shoulder, and carried it to the flock. This, too, said Jesus, represented the Realm of God in the heart of a man. If we lose courage, or happiness, or peace of mind, or self-respect, we are losing the Realm of God which ought to prevail in human hearts. There is but one course open to us and that is to backtrack to the point where we lost the precious possession and search until we find it again.

Suppose we have lost peace of mind. There is a reason for it. We ought not to lose it. If we have we ought to get it back. It is all wrong to be content with turmoil inside the heart. Everyone of us has the right to that inward peace subsisting at the heart of endless agitation. No things, no persons, outside ourselves were ever intended by the almighty Father to destroy the peace of mind of any of his children. Do things distress us, worry us, trouble us? Then we are submitting to the dominance of material things in our lives. We are like little children who kick at inanimate objects, bruise their shins against chairs, bite and scratch and pound tables and pianos because these material things in their obstinacy keep getting in the way. The children only hurt themselves. Having lost their peace of mind, they have not wisdom enough to go back where they lost it and find it again.

Do you say this is a foolish illustration and that grown men and women do not act in this way? Every day we see them act in this way. If you do not think that people allow themselves to be dominated by the material world, its gains and its losses, then answer me this: Did you ever see anybody who had lost peace of mind in the midst of luxury and riches drop the whole thing and go back to live in the little home "where we were so happy and so po' "? No, grown-up children are not in the habit of going back where they lost it to find their peace of mind.

> "I swear 'tis better to be lowly born,
>   And range with humble livers in content,
>   Than to be perked up in a glistering grief
>   And wear a golden sorrow."

Or suppose it is persons whom we allow to dominate us and filch away our calmness and content. There are hundreds of people who are permitting a querulous and impossible relative, a husband, a wife, a father or mother, a brother or sister, to invade their lives, cripple their freedom, and throw them into nervous spasms. Our relatives have a certain claim on us, but no one of them has sufficient claim to sap our individuality to its very foundations. "Honor thy father and thy mother" is a maxim as old as the nomad tribes, but in its name many a life has been crippled, crushed, and quenched. No foolish and selfish old man or woman has any right to destroy young, promising, and exuberant life. If the old person or the sick and querulous and utterly unreasonable relative cannot perceive that he is an incubus, then let the young and healthy and free put him where he ought to be, so that peace and calm may be the portion of the useful members of society.

Or perhaps the conflict that has destroyed peace of mind is entirely within. After all here are the bloodiest battle grounds of the soul. These inward contests, where in the dark corridors and chambers of the human heart rage the clash and clangor of sword and battle-ax on brand—here hopes and aspirations, promising powers and possibilities, lie wounded and bleeding. It is on this battle field that the dragon's teeth of the neuroses are sown—nervous prostration, hysteria, melancholia, and all the diseases of the mind. Have you such a conflict? Then quit it short, run away from it, get out of the battle smoke, go back to where you lost your peace of mind.

Perhaps self-respect has been lost. We have done what we ought not to have done, we have left undone what we ought to have done, and there is no health in us. Then the only sane and sensible thing to do is to rub out what is written on the page which has blurred the fine shimmer and sheen of our own just estimate of ourselves. Is it a habit which we think we cannot shake off? Then we are mistaken. We can go back to where we lost the good habit and, setting to work patiently and determinedly, we can undo the newer and more vicious set of habits and restore the older and simpler ones. Whatever else we lose, we cannot afford permanently to lose self-respect. It is the very Realm of God itself in the soul of a man; and we must go back and search till we find it.

Along with the loss of self-esteem and peace of mind goes the loss of courage. Be very sure, if you have lost courage, you lost it in the same place where you lost your peace of mind and your self-respect. These three belong together; the first two produce the last. The brave man is the one who thinks highly of himself, not more highly than he ought to think, but with a just and honest estimate of his own powers and limitations. The brave man is also serene, calm, at peace with himself and strong against the world. If you have lost that courage which once you had, then it is foolish to go on in the path you are treading. Go back where you lost it and find it again. In doing so one finds God; and with God inside him there is nothing that can make one afraid.

There was a man with thousands of enemies and only an occasional friend. He was arrested over and over, thrown into jail, put through the third degree, beaten with a cat-o'-nine-tails, knocked into insensibility with rocks and stones, shipwrecked time and again. But he kept going in spite of all obstacles, with disease constantly gnawing at his vitals, and accomplished the second most important piece of work this world has seen done. It was this man, Paul, who cried, ''I can do all things through Christ who strengtheneth me.''

We ought to be very certain, however, that the thing we have lost is indispensable, that it is a thing we can ever find again or cannot get along without, or for which there is no substitute. I was driving along in my motor car one time in western Kansas when a tire-ring flew off into the tall grass by the roadside. We searched carefully for several hundred yards but could not find it. Then we went on the rim to the nearest town about four miles ahead. At the garage there was no rim to fit; so the owner of the place said to me, ''You'd better go back where you lost it.'' I hired a flivver, went back, and the driver and I again searched for an hour or two. We never found it. The mechanic tried to make us a ring, but never succeeded. After a whole day lost, a philanthropic citizen of that blessed town took a ring off his own wheel that exactly fitted ours and lent it to the wayfarers. We then went on our way rejoicing.

Oftentimes there is a substitute for the thing you have lost, perhaps even better than the thing itself. We lose our innocence, inevitably lose it, and we sigh for the return of it all in vain. It is just as useless as it is natural for us to cry out at times,

"Backward, turn backward, O Time, in thy flight,
  Make me a child again, just for to-night."

Time is inexorable and will not turn back. We should like to pillow our heads in the innocence of childhood on our mothers' breasts, but it is not so ordered. In place of innocence there is a better thing obtainable, which is virtue—not to be blind to the evil but to see it, meet it, grapple with it, and overcome it. This is the high destiny of full-grown men and women.

Time takes from us, too, our illusions. Once we dreamed dreams and saw visions. Once all the world looked rosy and iridescent. Once we expected great things of life and could not brook disappointments. But life shattered our dreams, even the realization was not up to the expectation, while over and over again the realization itself was denied us. We were disappointed in people. They were not the wise, just, and kindly souls we had expected them to be. They were defective, angular, opinionated, selfish, and very, very foolish in our eyes. Our illusions were completely lost and gone. Then, if we were wise, we began to take the world as it comes, to take people as they are, to take life not as a dream but as a reality, and to see, maybe through tears, that with all its defects life is good, that with all faults people at heart are honest, aspiring, and kind. We began to see life steadily and to see it whole; we began even to prefer reality to illusion, the imperfect to the perfect, the stubborn and obstinate materials out of which all men and things are made as a challenge to our skill, our artistry, our wisdom, and our patience. Illusions are things well lost and not worth going back to find.

Nevertheless along with our innocence and our illusions sometimes goes our happiness. Is happiness a thing we would better lose? Not so, if it can be prevented. Happiness is a precious possession, a thing to be cherished and, if possible, held. Yet, when all is said and done, it is not an indispensable. One can get along without happiness. It is a by-product which in the nature of things ought to come to the honest, faithful workman, and by God's grace can come and usually does come to him who is faithful over a few things. But one can persevere, even in the midst of suffering, and, what is more, succeed in a worth-while piece of work, happiness or no happiness.

For centuries churches and theologians, preachers and evangelists, have used the words "convert" and "repent." If those words mean anything, they mean turn round, go back where you lost it, seek the precious coin or the lost sheep, which means the realm and the peace of God within the soul, until you find them. Those same theologians, however, have gone off on a wrong trail, I think, when they have insisted that man was originally sinful and bad. Original sin, the idea that our forefathers were vicious and wicked and that all we are partakers of their guilt from the hour of our birth, is a wicked and vicious old doctrine and utterly out of keeping with the truest philosophy and psychology. Man is not originally bad, but good. Jesus believed in nothing else quite so strongly as in the inherent goodness of human beings. Over and over again, with the utmost tenderness and compassion, he forgave men their sins and told them to go back and begin over again. No matter what the message of the theologian, this is the message of the Christ. He made no mistakes about human nature, about the wise and reasonable things for us to do. Through all the din and contention of the warring sects of the centuries, let us listen for the gentle voice of the Saviour of men; and if we are wandering in rough and rugged places, cutting ourselves with the stones and the thorns, let us turn back to the green pastures and the still waters where we may find peace of mind, self-respect, and courage, which mean for us the reign of God in our souls.

"I wish that there was some wonderful place
  Called the Land of Beginning Again,
 Where all our mistakes and all our heartaches
 And all of our poor foolish pain
 Could be dropped like a shaggy old coat at the door
  And never put on again.

XVII

THE WISDOM OF WILL ROGERS

Call for Samson that he may make us sport.
JUDGES 16: 25.

WE forget that, along with his other qualities, Samson, who at one time ruled Israel, established a reputation as a humorist. He played pranks on his enemies, the Philistines, such as tying the tails of foxes together, two by two, attaching a firebrand between the tails, and turning the animals loose in hostile cornfields. He proposed facetious riddles for the young men of the Philistines to solve. And in battle he grimly took the jawbone of an ass as a sword and killed thousands of them. Samson was a jokesmith with a great punch and an eye to public affairs.

Will Rogers, in our time, does not form an exact parallel to Samson; but I had to have a text. There are those who think that Mr. Rogers could be elected President of the United States, a judge in our Israel, or anything else he wanted to become, besides mayor of Beverly Hills, and that he would make a good President. I think he would be the first to know the impossibility of his election to high office. The American people takes itself too seriously. An avowed humorist they do not consider the right sort of person to put in high position. Witness such men as Tom Reed, Tom Marshall, and John Sharp Williams. They believe in electing men who never crack a smile and who look ponderous and wise. The masses love a humorist but want to keep him in his place. Will Rogers at this moment has more influence than any one of the last three Presidents during whose time he has flourished.

His history is perhaps well known. A cowboy of Oklahoma, with a keen eye to business, he made about twelve thousand dollars by the time he was twenty, near the end of the last century, and started out to see South America via New Orleans. Astonished at the bigness of that city, he decided to stop by London on his way to South America and see if it was bigger. He found a war breaking out in South Africa; so he volunteered in the British army, which found him handy with horses and set him to work to wrangle the herd at ten dollars a month. At the end of the war, finding that his skill with a rope intrigued the Britishers, he went with a circus in South Africa. Finally he landed in New York to do a vaudeville stunt with a rope.

Channing Pollock, with whom Will lived at that time in New York in an old tenement house, tells me that Rogers always wanted to speak some lines in his act, but Pollock felt that this awkward-looking cowboy, so skillful with a rope, probably would speak lines only very badly. One night Will got tangled in his rope on the stage and, grinning, muttered that a rope is a good thing to play with so long as you don't get it round your neck. The audience exploded with sudden laughter, and the manager rushed at him shouting, "Personality is your real line!" From then on he spoke whatever came into his head while twirling his rope, and began chewing gum to keep his throat from getting dry. His subsequent career we all know— Zeigfeld's Follies and a growing fame, until he made himself nationally known and beloved in four different fields: the stage, the movies, the radio, and the press.

I spent the greater part of a day with Will Rogers about 1919. He came to my office while I was in charge of a newspaper, and we called in two or three heads of departments, closed the doors, opened the windows, and spent two hours listening to him talk. He needed no spur except an occasional question or remark, but spun out his humor by the yard until our shouts of laughter must have been heard all over the business section of the city. Utterly spontaneous, his discourse could not have been prepared. That evening my wife and I dined with him and Otto Floto, the well-known sports writer, and Mrs.

Floto at the Muehlebach Hotel and watched the people dance. For two or three hours more, he kept up his flow of dry spontaneous humor. He is as full of it as an Oklahoma gusher is full of oil. The best things men do they do with the least effort.

Nevertheless, Will Rogers works hard. He travels all the time. Wherever there is trouble, he goes to it. Conscientiously he prepares himself for his observations on American life by becoming acquainted with his fellow citizens in every State in the Union. He knows America through and through, and knows how to put himself in the average American shoes and to speak the average American language. He can take such liberties with men in high position just because he does know the American mind so well. He declares that the reason he can poke fun at anybody, no matter how exalted, is because he doesn't advocate anything. He is not for this nor against that. He thinks that no man can be a humorist or even a philosopher and advocate causes. He believes that he is welcome to social converse with such men as President Coolidge, President Hoover, and Senator Borah, because they want to learn from him what America is thinking, and he has studied it to find out. He takes constantly the poses of illiteracy and ignorance; but we all know that he is far from ignorant, that he reads and studies widely, and that although he has had little schooling he has educated himself. His "Illiterate Digest," one of his books, bears only the outward marks of illiteracy.

Will Rogers fills a sorely needed place to-day more than he has at any time in his career. When people are depressed and unhappy they need a humorist more than at any other time. These are hard days for many people in America and throughout the world, days that try men's souls. Whoever shows them that they should not take themselves too seriously and should not take life somberly, serves as a public benefactor. We need entertainment; we need to see laughter holding both his sides; we need to make fun of ourselves and to make fun of life. Laughter is wholesome, produces sanity, clears the atmosphere, and purifies the blood. A man who laughs much or makes the world laugh much, helps to save the world. As some one has said, "Nobody ever plotted a crime while laughing." Religion itself, far from considering laughter incompatible, recognizes its value. The greatest saints I have known smiled much and even guffawed. Business men, who to-day are more heavily burdened and deeply perplexed than I have ever seen them, need men who can make them laugh so as to preserve their balance, their sanity of thinking, and keep them from destroying themselves in one way or another. Nobody can measure the service that Will Rogers is doing for the whole nation at this time of strain and stress.

Then we need somebody who will speak plainly to us, hold the mirror up to nature, help us to "see oursel's as ithers see us." One ancient emperor kept a man whose duty it was to remind his majesty every day that he was only human. Medieval kings all kept jesters close to the throne so that they should hear one voice which was not afraid to tell them the truth about themselves, to be honest and frank about affairs public and private. The American people need such a court jester lest we think too highly of ourselves. Will Rogers' statement, cabled from the Far East, is worth its weight in gold, to the effect that he thought the solution of the Philippine question is to turn the islands loose and then let them have a protectorate over the United States. In other words, while assuming to govern the Philippines until they come of age, we have made rather a mess of governing ourselves. Good for us to realize that, and to have somebody tell us that, without barb or a sting. You know, I am growing more and more to believe that the best way to cure anybody of faults is to laugh at him, provided you can laugh in such a way as not to anger him. That requires great skill. Not many can do it. I believe, for example, the best weapon against war is to laugh at its puffiness and pomp, its strutting and its false glory. I hope to see Will Rogers some day turn the blasts of laughter at the egregious god Mars.

Again, let us turn our attention to the large-hearted charity of our favorite humorist. When his friend, Fred Stone, is disabled in an airplane accident, Will Rogers takes his place upon the stage and plays, if not Fred's part, then his own part, until Fred is well again. When drought and famine visit the Southwest, Will Rogers goes everywhere over the region, flying back and forth, making speeches and campaigning for funds to relieve the suffering. Just before he started for Arkansas and Texas at that time, my wife telegraphed him at Washington, D. C., and asked him to come by here and make a speech for the benefit of the Women's Council of the Church, asking him what would be his fee. She hardly expected an answer, but soon got a long telegram saying that he would not have time to stop, but implying that at some other time he would come and that he would not charge her anything. That may have been just a courtesy, knowing that he could easily get out of it later on, but at all events it reveals the heart of the man. Of course, Will Rogers can command the highest prices in any of his four branches of expression, but he has appeared and spoken freely for

charitable purposes over and over again. No
man can be a wholesome and sane humorist
without a large sense of charity for his fellow
men.

Will Rogers' family life is known to all the
world. A showman practically ever since he
came of age, he is married to the same wife
after twenty-five or thirty years. Public opinion to the contrary notwithstanding, and in
spite of certain exhibitions in Hollywood, it
would not surprise me if the average of steadfast marriages among show people may not
measure up to about the average of the population in general. Anyway, Will Rogers bears
the reputation of a model husband and father.
He has been a companion to his children, and
even now they are his chief interest in life.
This fact helps him to reach the hearts of the
American people who still believe that the
family constitutes the unit of whatever civilization we may in the future hope to preserve.

Now I have only one quarrel with Will, and
that is over the matter of our foreign relations.
He says he stands for nothing, advocates no
cause. Well, I do. I stand for friendship with
the nations and I advocate the cause of greater
conciliation and coöperation with other nations.
Only so can we do the best for our own country.
And, honestly, I believe that Will does stand
for something and advocate something, even

though he does it unconsciously, and that is a policy of isolation and extreme nationalism. His utterances, even though jocular, point to a rather exaggerated Americanism, to a policy of every nation for itself and the devil take the hindmost. Let every people stew in its own juice and paddle its own canoe. I have never been able to understand this strain of thought in Will Rogers. He has traveled; he has been all over the world, you might say. And reading and thinking as he does, he should have learned that the whole world is one and that an exaggerated patriotism defeats itself. I cannot believe that Will Rogers takes the attitude of America first, right or wrong, just because that is the prevailing spirit of most of our people. He has shown himself brave enough to go against public opinion when he cared to. No, I am forced to the conclusion that, like many other public men, even of wide experience and knowledge, he is still essentially a Middle Westerner, isolated from the thought of the world, provincial, if you please, in outlook upon world affairs.

O well, there is no use being discouraged because America as a whole is thus circumscribed in its world outlook. We shall be forced, we are being forced, by the inexorable pressure of economic laws into world coöperation. When I saw the present Congress assembled and heard the blasts of provincialism, narrowness, and jingoism go up like a charivari on a rural wedding night, a wave of dismay came over me, and then I began to laugh. Let the little fellows toot their horns, I thought to myself, let them make all the noise they want to make to tickle the ears of their bucolic constituents. They are being swept along in spite of themselves toward reduction of war debts and reparations, reduction of tariffs and armaments, in the interest of self-preservation and in desperate attempts to restore economic well-being right here in America. They are like little chips being borne along on the breast of a swollen river. If the chips had voices, they would no doubt shout like those Congressmen to be taken ashore and to be saved from plunging over the falls into the big basin of international coöperation. But nothing on earth can save us from that plunge out of isolation into coöperation. I just wish Will Rogers knew it.

Nevertheless I love him, just as we all love him, for the full picture he presents—one of us, thoroughly American, just like a man off one of our farms, the kind of men we were brought up with. We love him for the laughter he has brought to us, for the plain and honest words he has spoken to us about ourselves, for the charity and helpfulness he has shown toward everybody needing help, from the lonely President in the White House down to the starving farmer in Arkansas river bottoms. We love him for his faithfulness to his friends and his affection for his family. We love him for his sanity and balance and poise.

He has the capacity for comradeship which after all is the essence of Christian ethics. I have no idea what Church, if any, Will Rogers belongs to. It's a matter of small moment to me. I hope he belongs to some Church, for every man ought to. With all its faults, the Church and what it stands for are the hope of the world. Nevertheless, I would rather see a man living out what Jesus stands for, even though outside the Church, than to see him in a Church and missing a thousand miles everything Jesus stood for. I think Will Rogers would be one of the first men on this continent that Christ would like to lock arms with if he should come here. He is the kind of man that the wholesome young Master of Nazareth sought out as his favorite comrades.

XVIII

AMOS 'N' ANDY

And Jonathan loved him as his own soul.
1 SAMUEL 18: 1.

SOME superior minds have formed a low estimate of American intelligence because Amos and Andy hold their place indefinitely as the most popular entertainers in our national life. These superior minds seem to be the same ones who had little use for Charlie Chaplin and Will Rogers; and if they had been alive at the time they would have looked with disdain upon Mark Twain.

I can join heartily with the intelligentsia who deprecate the advertising ballyhoo with which most of our radio entertainment is framed. I wish we could get along without it. But I have often wished that we had only the kernel of the walnut and not the shell. I have yearned for a pecan that had no hull and a coconut that was nothing but white meat and milk. Anyway, you can always sit by your radio instrument and tune out the ballyhoo until the real artists come on. For one, I am willing to crack the nut, take off the hull, and get at the sweet meat of Harlem.

For myself, I consider Amos and Andy wholesome, entertaining, and instructive. I am glad not to be so sophisticated nor so mentally elevated that I cannot get a good bedtime story from them every evening of the week. Either a very strict censorship exists in that broadcasting station in New York, or else Amos and Andy don't need any censorship. Nothing off color, nothing profane, nothing even coarse comes over the air during their fifteen minutes.

Moreover, the artistic skill of the two men who present this entertainment excites constant wonder. They enact the part of a dozen different persons, maybe more, but only the two voices come on the radio. How versatile those voices and how vivid the impression they give of several people moving about in the Fresh Air Taxicab office, in the lunch room, in the court, by the lake in the summer time, and for a while in the jail. How much human nature, grave and gay, these two artists pack into those short broadcasts. How their speech has entered into the vernacular of the American people! The highest paid entertainers in the world? Very well, I am inclined to think they deserve it. The devoted friendship between Amos and Andy compares favorably with the historic friendships between any two men, running clear back to the time of David and Jonathan whose souls were knit together with a love passing the love of women. And probably David and Jonathan were of about the same complexion as Amos and Andy.

I have heard that some colored people—again, I fancy, among the intelligentsia—disapprove of this broadcast because they think it holds their race up to ridicule. I do not believe they ought to be sensitive about it any more than the Scotch people should be sensitive concerning the jokes at the expense of their nation, or the Irish, or the Kentucky mountaineers, or the Jewish people, or any of the rest of us who have interesting and amusing ways and manners. Whatever fun can be got out of each other harmlessly and good-humoredly in this sad old world, we ought to get and add to the gayety of nations. There is far too little laughter, and far too little love, and far too little sense of humor, in a rather melancholy world. It is quite possible to become so sophisticated that we can take ourselves too seriously. America by and large, I think, does not suffer from this trait. Kipling says of the American, "Mine ancient humor saves him whole." A man is greatly handicapped in living his life, let alone in carrying on a career, without a sense of humor. Difficult for married people to live together and for parents to bring up children without a sense of humor. So I am sorry for people who cannot love Mark Twain, Will Rogers, Charlie Chaplin, and Amos and Andy.

At one time poor little Amos struggled in the toils of the law and experienced for the first time in his life what the average Negro dreads beyond anything except a hospital, the bars of a prison. He had a taste of the third degree, and the weakness of circumstantial evidence. I note that the president of the International Association of Chiefs of Police protested against the portrayal of that third degree given in this broadcast and denied that such methods are in use. Over against his authority, plainly interested, I would cite the authority of Zechariah Chafee, Jr., in the *Atlantic Monthly*, who reveals what is common knowledge to most police reporters of newspapers, that the third degree is undoubtedly practiced in most American cities. Mr. Chafee adds that certain of the larger cities, like Boston, Cincinnati, and Philadelphia, no longer use it and have found that they get better results by kindly and sympathetic questioning. Of course, the use of the rubber hose, the beating up of prisoners to get confessions, all the cruelty exercised upon a suspect, can be so covered up that the general public seldom has an opportunity to get at the real facts. It is difficult to convince most of us that the third degree is not practiced. I am well aware of the justification often uttered in behalf of it, that the police are dealing with hardened and lawless men and have to fight fire with fire. Nevertheless, the quick denial of this president of chiefs of police testifies sufficiently to an uneasy conscience on the subject. If the third degree does exist, as most of us believe it does, it is one more instance of man's inhumanity to man.

As a matter of fact, we have made very little progress in our treatment of the criminal. We have done but very little studying of scientific penology. We have a long way to go in getting at the minds and the motives of criminal men and women. Hard for us to realize that the so-called underworld, and even the thousands of men in the prisons, are for the most part just young men, like all other young men, whom fortune has played a tragic trick, but who differ no whit from our own sons and daughters. But for the grace of God, any one of them might have been your son or mine. To reclaim and rehabilitate these young people and make them useful members of society should be the end and aim of our penology. Even Russia at this hour is giving us lessons in the treatment of the criminal.

We have long laid too much emphasis upon property as compared with human life. Things never for a moment weigh in the scale in value with men and women. No machine, however expensive, compares with the value of the man's life who runs that machine. Yet our industry takes more care of the machine than of the man. None of our institutions, banks, courts, stores, skyscrapers, corporations, none of our intricate organizations and propertied interests, can rival in value the lives of men and women; yet our society is organized as if property were the most important thing on earth. If Jesus could say, and meet the approval of the world as he does, "The Sabbath was made for man, not man for the Sabbath," then we ought to be able to say, "The mill was made for man and not man for the mill." Until we shall have learned so simple and self-evident a truth as that, we shall not be in the way of solving the problems of our civilization.

One other thing worth our learning from Amos and Andy is that all human life is interesting to those who have eyes to see and ears to hear. Not merely rich people, nor white-collared people, nor even educated people, may hold much charm for us. The most ordinary people may hold much charm for us. The most ordinary people we come into contact with often present the greatest interest and the most natural human charm. Believe me, Madam, you might get an infinite amount of stimulus from your cook, just as some of the rest of us get it from our barbers, from the men we meet

in the barber-shop chairs or in the corner drug
store. If you want illustration of this, read the
books of David Grayson, that star reporter, and
see what he learned from the bootblack, the
janitor, the farmer, the Scotch preacher, and,
not to leave him out, the millionaire. Read the
books of anybody who is a master of the literary
art and see how the common people fill his
pages and fill his mind. It is never the real
intelligentsia, but only the false, educated beyond their intellect, who disdain the humble
people like those who circle round the Fresh Air
Taxicab office.

They are imperfect, that little bunch of Har-
lemites, but who is not imperfect? They hold
the mirror up to nature in masterful fashion to
show us the imperfections in which we all share.
Andy, with his illusions of grandeur, as he
counts his income tax and as he boasts and
swaggers, exaggerates, and puts on airs—how
many business men does he satirize without
sting and without malice! In a much kindlier
way he does what Sinclair Lewis did with Bab-
bitt, and probably much more effectively just
because all bitterness is left out. You can never
reform and sweeten human life by hate, like
the hatreds of Lewis; but you can with gentle
humor like that of Andy. Then there is Amos,
forever struggling against untoward circumstances, but with a clear mind that sees through

all sham, pretense, and chicanery. It is hard to get the best of Amos, harmless and kindly as he is. Andy is forever taken in by any blusterer that comes along; never Amos.

Then the women in the party: Madam Queen, the gold digger; the battle-ax; and Mrs. Crawford, who is always very unhappy. We have known a few women like these three. Then there's Ruby Taylor and Aunt Lillian. Thank God, we have known a few, yes, a great many women as good and kind. Then Mrs. Van Porter, who carries her spectacles on a stick, called, according to the Kingfish, a longnet, and who can't see through them but looks over the top of them and around them all the time. We've seen a few women like that. And Lightnin'. I've known one or two white men just as slow, as lazy, as futile. O yes, there's a picture gallery here in which most of us can find ourselves. It is the humble people, whether of Drumtochty or of Harlem, that present fascinating images of all mankind.

Then there is the undying truth and loyalty among this little group of people. They quarrel with each other, they try to get money away from each other, they try to outshine each other; but when it comes to the hard pinch of life, they stand by each other and work for each other. I don't know how we are to solve our social problems on any other basis. It has seemed to me through the long observation of the years that the humbler people, the poorer people, are the ones who know most about loyalty and helpfulness to one another in the trials of life. They share with one another as we more comfortable people do not incline to do. Maybe it is because they know from experience what it means to be in hard lines and therefore their sympathies and their helpfulness can more easily be summoned. Whatever the reason, certain it is that those on the verge of direst poverty share and share alike with each other.

We are accustomed to speak with condescension of the life philosophy of the colored race. We say that they are naturally so happy that privation means little to them, and that this easy irresponsible contentment accounts for the backward condition of their race. I rather think that our attitude should be not one of condescension but of emulation and aspiration. We are not so happy as they are. With all its lack of sanitation, the Negro quarters, whether in this city or in Harlem, holds more of the real joy of life than our boulevards or Riverside Drive or Park Avenue. It were better for us if we could catch something of the independence of mere things, something of the joy in song, in human association, in conversation, in worship, that characterizes these humble people who possess so much freer spirits and deeper philosophy of living than we possess. They can meet hard times because they are used to hard times. They can be happy with little things, because their lives consist not in the abundance of the things they possess. If they are careless and carefree, then they are teaching us a lesson, because we certainly are anxious for the morrow. Better for us if we laughed and sang more, got together and talked and warmed up toward each other more, if we congregated and worshiped together more.

It is a Christian philosophy after all. It is the simple life that Jesus came to teach. He came to make life brighter, happier, more carefree. He said, "My joy I leave with you." He taught a fine carelessness when he said, "Consider the lilies." He meant for us to toss our heads and wear whatever colors came to us, in any breeze, with the careless brightness of the flowers. The Harlem people know how to do that as the rest of us do not.

Then he taught us to take life as it comes, to adapt ourselves to it, to meet storms with courage and sunshine with happiness. His was a robust view of life, strong, courageous, and radiant. Relaxed? Yes, with the relaxation of the athlete whom blows cannot crush just because he is relaxed.

Then what higher thing did he teach us than

affection for one another and loyalty to one another? There cannot be loyalty where the affections are not involved. We see people violating the loyalties of life all round us all the time. They fail of loyalty to their church, to their families, to their city, to their friends, just because they are lacking in the emotion which engenders loyalty. How can they be loyal when their hearts have never been touched? Only affection brings unswerving loyalty. Love, the greatest thing in the world, the very top of Jesus' teaching, affection in all our relationships—this we can learn from the humblest people more often than from the richest and most aristocratic. This we can learn among the warrens of the poor in any city from here to Harlem.